You Can F***ing Do This!

A simple journal for awareness, presence and real life.

REBECCA LAZZELLE

You Can **F***ing** Do This!

Published by
Illumify Media Global
www.IllumifyMedia.com
"Let's bring your book to life!"

Hardback ISBN: x

Typeset by Art Innovations (http://artinnovations.in/)
Cover design by Debbie Lewis

Printed in the United States of America

"The journey of
a thousand miles
begins with a single
step."

— Lao Tzu

Contents

A friend of mine bought me a journal for my birthday a few years ago. I wasn't and still am not really a traditional journaler. I try to jot down at least one thing I'm grateful for every day, but I've never really journaled. I don't know why.

After my life as I knew it fell apart, I dropped my gratitude practice in favor of survival. I found myself needing something else, and one night picked up the small, prompted journal I got from my friend and started writing. Some prompts were helpful, others I hated. I worked through that journal for months. It wasn't perfect, though in a time of great despair, it helped me.

The following pages contain a variety of insights and activities I came across on my healing journey that I want to share with you. The goal is exposure not mastery, trying new things rather than expecting something different from your existing behavior. The activities don't need to be done in any particular order. You might find yourself drawn to one and hating another and that's ok too.

The first part of the journal contains all the activities. Once you find one you like, there is an opportunity for you to turn that particular activity into thirty days of curiosity and reflection. One small change in your life may be all the catalyst you need for other changes that are grounded in the self, presence, and mindfulness in this crazy world we live in.

Curiosity is just that. Small daily opportunities to connect with yourself, remember your worth, and move forward. Try one, try them all, it's totally up to you.

This is a space for curiosity, growth, trying new things, self-compassion, and grace. If you start the thirty days, and it's just not resonating, it's okay to stop. You tried it and now you're moving on. If you start and get distracted for a few days, that's okay too. Look at you! You came back to it! Hopefully you feel proud of that.

Deep breaths. You already took the first step; you bought this journal. You gave the universe your intention. What a great start!

PS: I wanted to say a special thank you to the friends and family that made this journal a reality. Thank you, Shannon, you are the best sister anyone could have asked for. Thank you, Jermaine, your ongoing support is unmatched. Thank you, Andre, your continued belief in me is truly appreciated. And thank you, AJ, your honesty and connection is something I will forever cherish.

"All that we are is the result of what we have thought; it is founded on our thoughts and made up of our thoughts."

— Buddha

If you've picked up this journal, you're interested in self-change, maybe even self-transformation. We won't go all the way to transformation yet. Small steps first. Maybe you've already started to feel subtle shifts in yourself, your outlook, or your world recently, and you're ready to move in that direction. Maybe you don't know where or how to start and are looking for ideas.

Are you feeling the desire for something new? Why is this important to you now?

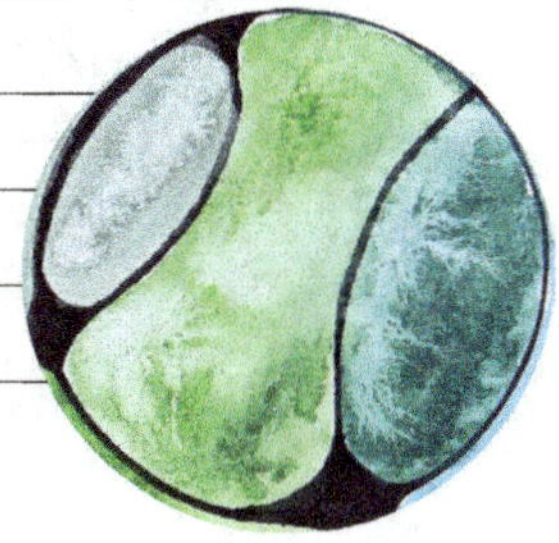

"Out of suffering have emerged the strongest souls; the most massive characters are seared with scars."

— Kahlil Gibran

It takes courage to make changes in your life. It takes bravery to try something new and step into the unknown. It takes confidence to be uncomfortable.

What does courage mean to you? Why is it important in your life?

Are there changes in your life you'd like to make that feel uncomfortable? Why do you think that is?

A Little Dabbling

Before committing to anything new, it helps to experiment.

This section is an invitation to try different mindfulness and awareness practices in small, simple ways. The next fifteen activities give you a chance to explore what grounding, noticing, and being present might look like in real life.

Some of these might resonate right away. Others might feel awkward, boring, or surprisingly helpful. That's normal. The goal is simply to notice what shifts when you give your attention to something on purpose.

Mindfulness isn't a one-size-fits-all experience. Different practices land differently for different people, and sometimes the ones that help the most are the ones we didn't expect to enjoy.

Try things. See what you like. Skip what you don't. There's nothing to perfect here. Just curiosity.

"Spend the afternoon. You can't take it with you."

— Annie Dillard

Grounding

When you touch the earth with your bare skin, this is grounding.

The earth's surface contains a vast supply of free electrons producing a natural negative charge. When we connect with the earth directly, those electrons may react with our own positively charged free radicals that may allow our human forms to sync with the natural frequencies of the earth.[1] Many people say grounding helps them feel more connected, present, and attuned to the natural world.

Some grounding researchers suggest a direct correlation between the widespread use of insulating materials, such as synthetic rubber in modern shoes, and chronic inflammation in our society.

While you may feel an instant calming or depth, research into grounding continues to evolve. Some grounding researchers propose that grounding for twenty minutes may even reduce the effects of things like jet lag.

The more time you spend connected to the earth, the more opportunity your physical body has to reconnect and return toward homeostasis.

Reading about grounding is one thing. Experiencing it is another. Take a few moments to complete the Grounding Activity on the following page.

Grounding Activity

Audio instructions

1. Step outside.
2. Remove your shoes and socks.
3. Step onto the earth.
4. Notice how you feel.
5. Remain standing, sit down, or lie down. Make sure your skin is touching the earth.
6. Close your eyes.
7. Stay connected to Mama Gaia for fifteen minutes.

How did you feel the moment you touched the earth?

How did you feel after the fifteen minutes?

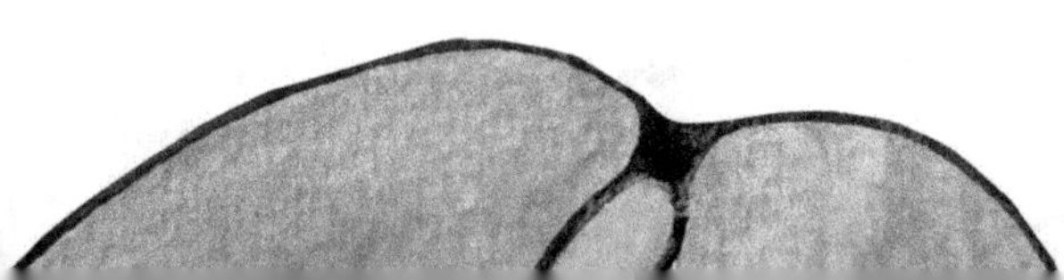

"Obstacles are those frightful things you see when you take your eyes off your goal."

— Henry Ford

Just Breathe

Breathing. We do it, all day, all night, every day. Most of the time it's run by our autonomic nervous system, automatic in the background, without our awareness.

When our breathing goes tight and shallow, as it can during moments of anxiety or panic, the sympathetic nervous system, the fight or flight response, becomes active. Slow, deep breathing, on the other hand, activates the parasympathetic nervous system, increasing relaxation and calm.

Intentional and conscious breathing allows for an opportunity to pause, collect ourselves, calm the mind, and reconnect with the present moment. In my experience, intentional and focused breathing can help interrupt the free-fall of a panic attack. It may also promote completion of the ninety-second physiological emotional processing wave, as described by Dr. Jill Bolte Taylor.[2]

Some researchers suggest deep breathing, using your diaphragm, can directly and indirectly affect your central nervous system[3] and others propose this type of breathing may actually decrease stress.[4]

Even a few minutes of conscious breathing can begin to shift how the body feels. Let's take a few moments now to reconnect with your breath.

Just Breathe Activity

Audio instructions

Get comfortable, you will be in this position for two minutes.

1. Close your eyes.
2. Breathe in through your nose for a count of four.
3. Breathe out of your mouth for a count of four.
4. Do this for about one minute.
5. Now, place your hand on your belly and direct the breath there.
6. Breathe in through your nose for a count of four.
7. Breathe out of your mouth for a count of four.
8. Do this for about one minute.
9. Open your eyes.

How did that feel?

"We are not born to be, but to grow."

— Margaret Fuller

Box Breathing

Box breathing in a simple, structured technique. Practices involving controlled and extended breaths can be traced back thousands of years to pranayama, an ancient yogic tradition focused on extending breath and cultivating prana, often described as life-force energy.

The modern term **box breathing** was popularized by Navy SEAL trainer Mark Divine in the mid-2000s as a way to describe the equal-count breathing cycle: inhale, hold, exhale, and hold, each for the same length of time. It is believed to improve concentration, lower blood pressure, and calm the nervous system.

Like other specific breathing techniques, box breathing is intentional and conscious, allowing for an opportunity to pause, collect ourselves, calm the mind, and reconnect with the present moment.

Let's take a few minutes to experiment with this particular breathing practice.

Box Breathing Activity

Audio instructions

1. Sit upright.
2. Slowly inhale through your nose, to the count of four.
3. Hold your breath for another slow count of four.
4. Slowly exhale through your mouth to the count of four, expelling all the air from your lungs and abdomen.
5. Hold your breath for another slow count of four.
6. Repeat four more times.

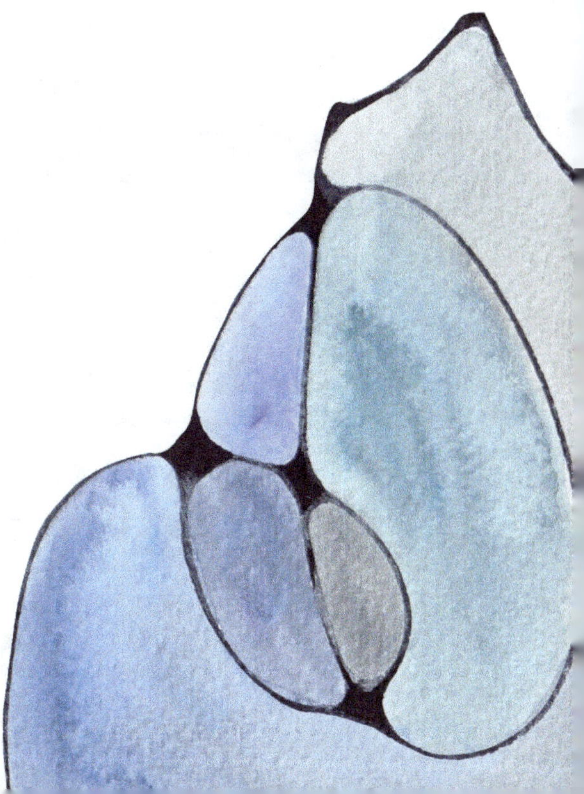

How did that feel?

"It is impossible
for a man to learn
what he thinks
he already knows."

— Epictetus

Short Grounding Meditation

Meditation is the practice of gently returning your attention to the present moment and becoming familiar with your natural state of awareness. It is not about stopping thoughts or necessarily emptying the mind.

Meditation has a history spanning thousands of years. While it has traditionally been associated with spiritual practices, modern scientific research offers additional insight to why people turn to meditation today. Ongoing studies suggest that meditation may actually physically rewire the brain, a process known as neuroplasticity.

Through meditation, thoughts, emotions, and sensations are allowed to move through the brain without resistance, while you learn to rest in a deeper sense of presence and stability beneath them. The practice is about "coming back," returning your attention again and again with patience and curiosity.

Over time, meditation helps anchor you back into yourself, creating space between experience and reaction, and allowing life to be met with greater clarity, calm, and awareness.

Silent meditation has not worked for me, at least not yet. I prefer guided meditations or meditations with music, which provide just enough structure for my hyperactive brain to settle and connect.

I hope you will enjoy the short grounding meditation offered here.

Short Grounding Meditation Activity

Audio instructions

1. Sit down (on a chair, on the floor, on the couch) and keep your back straight and relaxed.
2. Close your eyes.
3. Breathe consciously, paying attention to each inhale and exhale for a minute or two.
4. Imagine a root extending from your body into the earth, down, down, down through the layers of the earth, all the way to the center of the earth where there is a crystal. The root wraps around that crystal and then travels up through the layers of the earth to connect with your body.
5. When the connection is made you feel a settling, a calming, a connection.
6. Breathe consciously, paying attention to each inhale and exhale for another minute or two.

What kind of crystal did you find? What does that mean to you?

How do you feel?

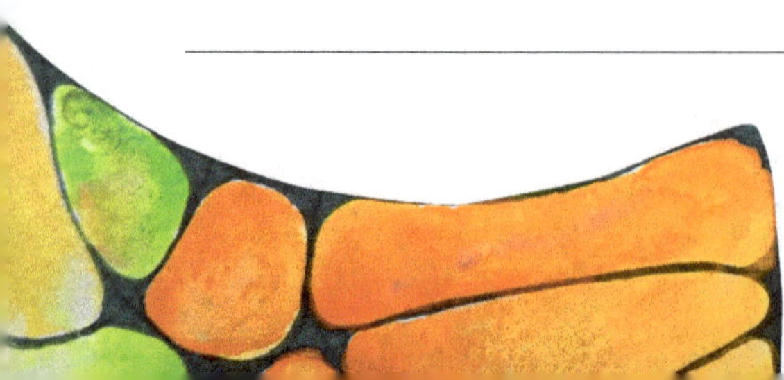

"It's no use going back to yesterday, because I was a different person then."

— Lewis Carroll

Senses Grounding Practice

Sometimes the mind travels far ahead or far behind, replaying what has already happened or trying to solve what hasn't yet arrived. When that happens, the body often follows, tightening, bracing, or drifting away from the present moment.

The senses grounding practice, commonly known as the 5-4-3-2-1 grounding technique, is a simple way to gently return to where you are right now. By intentionally noticing what you can see, feel, hear, smell, and taste, your attention shifts from racing thoughts back into the physical world.

This practice helps reduce stress, anxiety, and overthinking by engaging all five senses in the here and now. As your focus moves toward concrete sensory details, the nervous system begins to step out of fight-or-flight mode and back toward regulation.

This practice does not require silence, special tools, or perfect focus. It can be done anywhere, whether you are sitting at home, walking outside, or moving through a busy day. Each time you pause to notice your senses, you give your mind and body a moment to reset.

Start slowly. Let curiosity lead. Over time, this practice can become a familiar doorway back to steadiness, presence, and yourself.

Senses (5-4-3-2-1) Gounding Activity

Take a deep breath. Work through each sense, one at a time.

Audio instructions

5. **See five things around you.** Look closely at your surroundings: the texture of the ground, the way light shines on an object, or the specific colors around you.
4. **Feel four sensations.** Pay attention to physical sensations. How do your clothes feel on your skin? Is there pressure in your body where you're connecting with the ground or furniture?
3. **Hear three distinct sounds.** Close your eyes and tune in to the sounds around you. Appliances humming? Distant traffic? Birds chirping?
2. **Smell two things.** What do you smell? Fresh air? The absence of anything in particular?
1. **Taste one thing.** Any lingering flavors in your mouth? The absence of a specific taste is still something.

Write down your observations:

How do you feel?

Which sense was the most difficult? Why do you think that is?

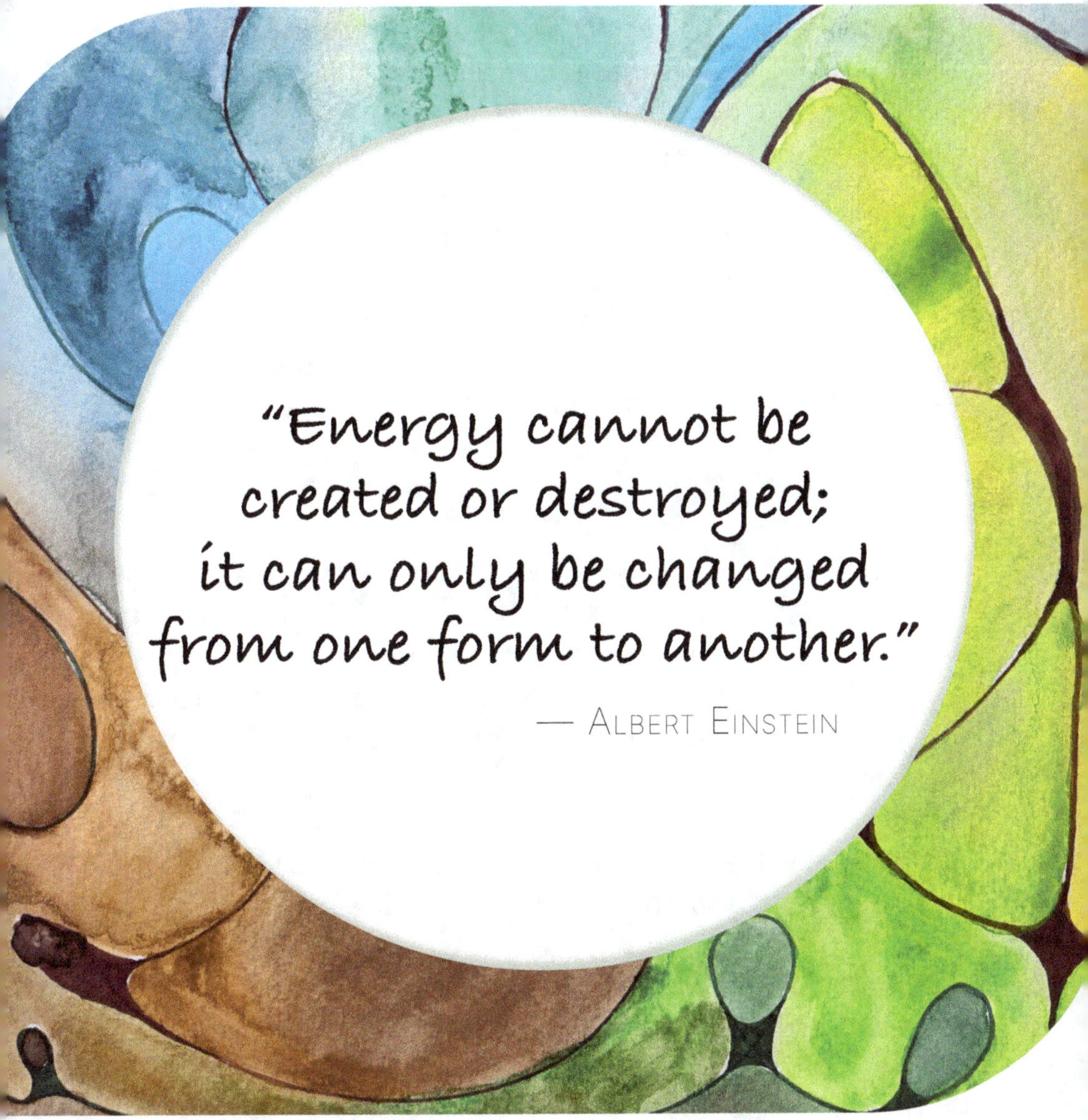

"Energy cannot be created or destroyed; it can only be changed from one form to another."

— Albert Einstein

Dance

Long before dance became something I did, it was simply something humans did together. Across cultures and throughout history, people have moved their bodies to celebrate, to grieve, to connect, and to come back to themselves. Dance was never about looking good. It was about feeling alive.

Modern research now echoes what many traditions have always known: Rhythmic movement paired with music helps regulate the nervous system. Dancing releases endorphins and oxytocin, lowers stress hormones like cortisol, and can shift the brain into a flow state where anxiety softens and connection increases. Movement gives the body a way to discharge excess energy that words alone cannot reach.

As discussed in my Spirituality, What? conversation (QR code link below) with movement facilitator Malaika Darville, dance creates a space where judgment fades and expression takes over. When people move freely together, something changes. The mind quiets and lets the body lead. Community forms naturally through shared rhythm and presence.

And yes, it can feel strange at first. We're adults. We've learned to be self-aware, controlled, and composed. Fuck that!

Start small. Sway. Stretch. Walk to the rhythm of a song you love. Let your body move before your mind decides whether it should.

Dance Activity

Audio instructions

Rebecca's YouTube Playlist

Spirituality, What? Podcast about Dance

1. Pick a song.
2. Dance to it unabashedly! (Close your eyes if you need to.)

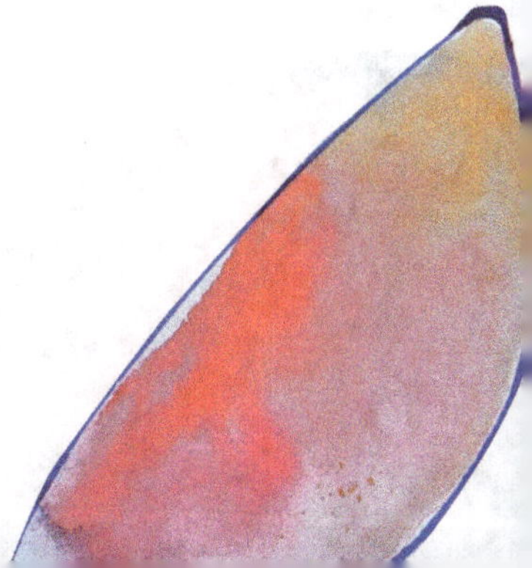

Which song did you pick? Why?

How do you feel?

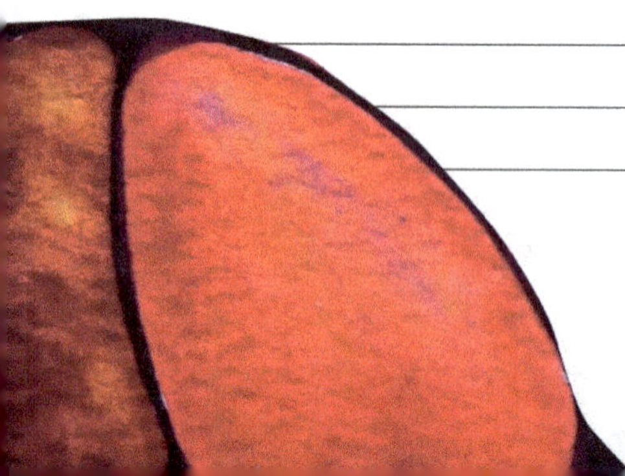

"Gratitude is magical because the more you practice it, the more things you can be grateful for."

— Iris Angellys

Gratitude

I started my gratitude journaling practice years ago. A beautiful red leather journal caught my eye on a trip to India, and that was it.

Gratitude is the practice of consciously recognizing and feeling appreciation for what already exists, down to the smallest aspects of life, in a way that restores presence and shifts perception toward abundance. It reconnects a person to themselves and something larger.

More than simply saying thank you, gratitude is an emotional and relational experience. It invites us to notice goodness and to acknowledge that many of the things sustaining us come from beyond our own effort, fostering connection, humility, and a deeper sense of belonging. Over time, practicing gratitude strengthens our capacity to experience joy, even alongside uncertainty or difficulty, by training the mind to remain open to what is still working, still meaningful, and still alive in the moment.

Gratitude activates different regions of the brain than stress. Brain imaging studies show increased activity in the prefrontal cortex and reward pathways—the areas associated with positive emotion, social bonding, and resilience—when we feel gratitude.[5]

Research suggests that focusing on being grateful can lower cortisol levels, reduce blood pressure, and support overall nervous system regulation.

Let's take a few minutes to settle into gratitude.

Gratitude Activity

Audio instructions

1. Think about some things you might be grateful for: your eyes, to witness the beauty of this world or a smile on a loved one's face or your strong legs that get you around. We can be grateful, even for the little things.
2. Write down three to five deeply felt positive experiences, people, or moments that you are grateful for.

What are a few things you are grateful for right now?

How does thinking about things you could be grateful for make you feel?

"The artist must not only train his eye but also his soul."

— Clara Schumann

Coloring

Coloring is often associated with childhood, yet many people rediscover it later in life as a quiet and surprisingly powerful way to slow down. When you color, your attention naturally settles into the present moment. The simple act of choosing colors and filling shapes gives the mind something gentle to focus on, allowing the body to soften out of stress and mental overload.

Research shared by the Mayo Clinic Health System suggests that coloring can calm the brain and support relaxation by shifting attention away from worry and toward steady, repetitive movement. As focus narrows to the page in front of you, heart rate and breathing may slow, and the nervous system begins to move out of a stress response and into a more regulated or meditative state. Many people notice improved sleep, reduced anxiety, and an overall sense of ease after even short periods of creative focus.

Coloring engages both analytical and creative parts of the brain at the same time. This balanced activity encourages a relaxed but alert state similar to meditation or flow, where self-conscious thoughts quiet and time feels less urgent.

There is no right way to color. Stay inside the lines or don't. Choose colors intentionally or randomly. Let the experience be simple.

Coloring Activity

1. Grab some markers, pens, pencils, crayons, paints, whatever you'd like.
2. Spend fifteen minutes coloring the following image.

Audio instructions

How do you feel after coloring the image?

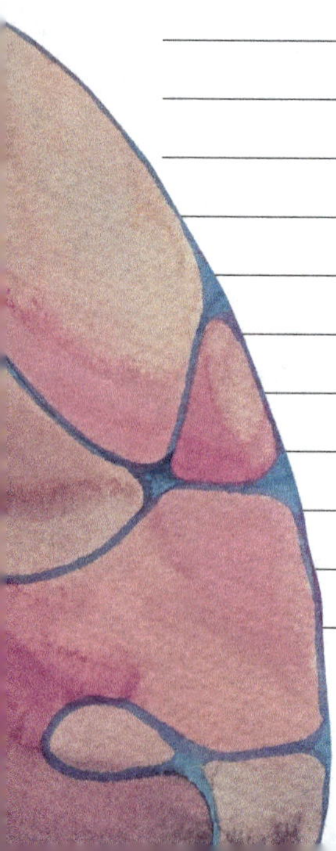

"Good food is the foundation of genuine happiness."

— Auguste Escoffier

Mindful Eating

Years ago I spent twenty-five minutes eating a single raisin, and it changed everything for me. Later, I tried the same exercise with generic candies and junk foods I thought I loved. It turns out, many were utterly disappointing.

Food and nourishment are essential to our experience here on this planet, yet so much of our eating happens on autopilot. How many times have you sat in front of a screen, finished a meal, and realized you barely remember tasting it? It's happened to me.

We're too hungry, too tired, too busy, the reasons are endless. Eating becomes another task to complete rather than an experience of true nourishment to notice.

Mindful eating invites something different. We slow down and become aware again. When we pay attention, food often tastes different. Sometimes better. Sometimes not at all like we expected.

Mindful eating is about curiosity. It's about learning what your body actually enjoys, what satisfies you, and what leaves you feeling supported rather than depleted.

For the next few minutes, you'll be invited to experience food slowly, intentionally, and with full attention.

Mindful Eating Activity

Audio instructions

1. Get a raisin or some other food you can hold in your hand.
2. Spend a few minutes looking at the food. What color is it? How does it look in the light versus the shade? How does it look compared to different surfaces and objects around you? How does it look close up vs. far away?
3. Spend a few minutes feeling the food. What does it feel like in your hand? What does it feel like between your fingers? If you apply a little bit of pressure how does that feel?
4. Spend a few minutes listening to the food. With it between your fingers put it close to your ear? What do you hear?
5. Spend the few minutes smelling the food. Place it in your hand and put it close to your nose. How does it smell? What happens if you close your eyes? Does it smell differently in each nostril? How does this smell compare to any other time you may have eaten this same food?
6. Spend a few minutes tasting the food (don't eat it yet). Place it on your tongue. What does it taste like? If you pull your tongue in your mouth and close it, how does that change the flavor? Move it around in your mouth. Do you notice anything about how the flavor changes in different parts of your mouth?
7. Now bite down! Chew slowly, savoring the flavor. What is that like?

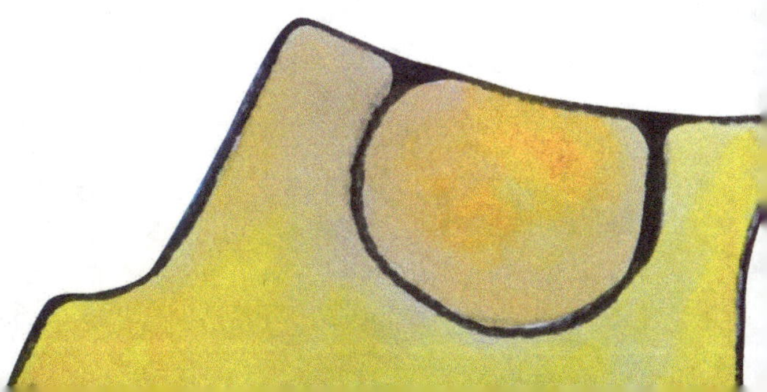

How did that activity change your perspective about raisins (or whatever food you tried)?

How do you feel having thought about what you are tasting and eating?

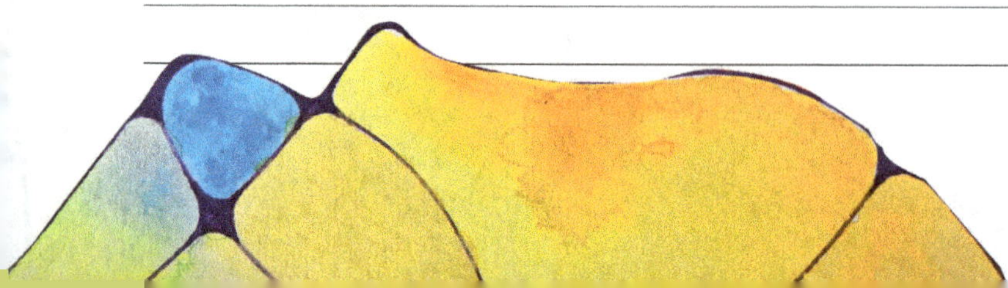

"The health of the body depends largely upon the health of the soul."

— Ellen G. White

Mindful Chewing

Like mindful eating, chewing more is one way to slow down and eat with more awareness.

The idea of chewing food slowly isn't new. In the early 1900s, health reformer Horace Fletcher encouraged people to chew each bite thoroughly to slow eating and increase awareness.

Modern research suggests that chewing more slowly can reduce overall calorie intake, improve body signals of fullness, and slow your overall eating pace.

Digestion starts in the mouth and not the stomach, chewing thoroughly gives your body time to recognize nourishment before it reaches your stomach. As you slow down, flavors often change, preferences become clearer, and eating becomes less automatic and more intentional.

Let's give it a try.

Diary of a CEO Podcast episode referencing chewing

Mindful Chewing Activity

Audio instructions

1. Grab some food.
2. Take a bite and chew it forty times.
3. Try another one.
4. Try a different food.
5. If you're trying this during a meal, set your cutlery down after each bite.

The actual goal isn't counting chews; it's simply remembering to notice.

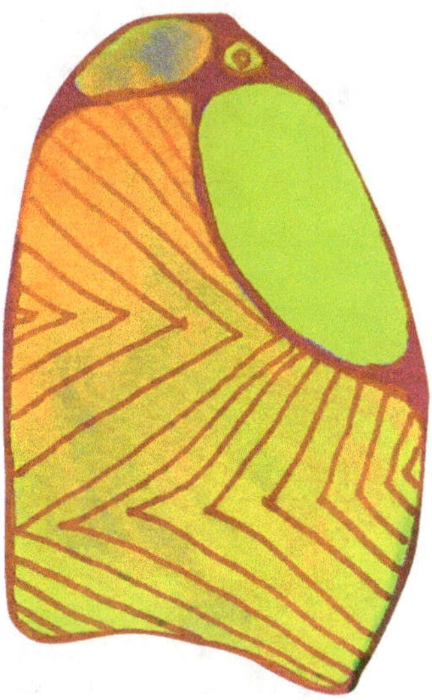

How did that feel? What thoughts did you have while doing the activity?

"The self is made, not given."

— Barbara Myerhoff

Affirmations

Affirmations are interesting. The Oxford dictionary defines affirmation as emotional support or encouragement and the action or process of affirming something. Self-affirmation is more than positive thinking. Neuroscience research shows that reflecting on core values activates brain networks involved in motivation, meaning, and planning. Practiced consistently, affirmations help the nervous system shift from defense toward growth.[6] Research even suggests affirmations can influence action, not just mood. They help the brain notice something different than the default.

To the universe, thoughts are as real as spoken words, and apparently it has a hard time understanding *not*. As with any creative processes, affirmations require practice to master, but as long as we aren't in survival mode, once we master affirmations, we can change ourselves and our reality with the way we think.

Daily affirmations, like other mindfulness practices, create a space for slowing down and connecting with ourselves. Even if affirmations don't feel true at first, they effectively sink in through repetition.

Let's give it a try.

Affirmation Activity

Audio instructions

1. Think of an affirmation you can tell yourself. Here are some examples
    a. I am loved unconditionally.
    b. I alone hold the truth of who I am.
    c. I am worthy.
    d. I am open to healing.
    e. I am a radiant being of light, fully one with the infinite universe.
2. Stand infront of the mirror, or close your eyes, whichever you prefer.
3. Place your hand on your heart.
4. Slowly and with intention say the affirmation.
5. Pause.
6. Repeat the affirmation three to five more times, settling into the feeling and calmness of the present moment.

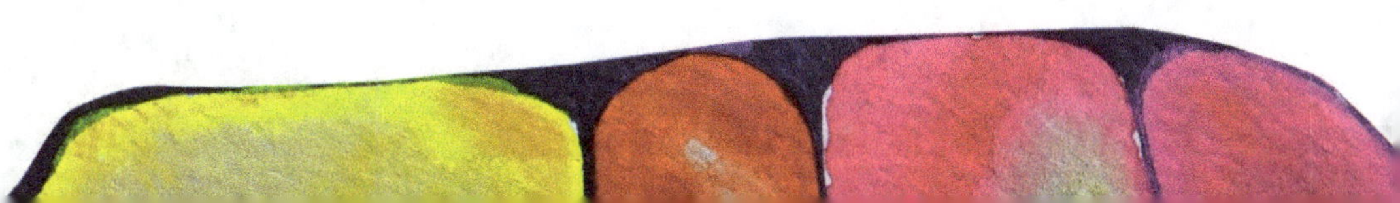

Which affirmation(s) did you choose?

How did that feel? What did you notice? Write down any comments, thoughts or notes you have about the experience.

"The more clearly you understand yourself and your emotions, the more you become a lover of what is."

— Baruch Spinoza

Choosing In

Ever had the experience where you made a choice, or committed to something and later found yourself questioning why you did that?

Choosing in (or out) is about making conscious and intentional choices. So many of us are running on autopilot or doing things out of habit or even tradition that we may not take a conscious moment to choose in and understand how we truly feel about something.

In some cases we may feel forced to choose a certain way. Taking a moment to understand the factors that lead to our choices, evaluate our position, and consciously move forward in a particular direction gives us more ownership and acceptance of the choices in our lives. We stop feeling like the victims and start acting like the creators we are.

With conscious choice we are not necessarily choosing based on fantasy, avoidance, fear or pressure, or even unconscious conditioning.

A conscious choice begins when we slow down enough to see reality clearly not the version shaped by comparison or avoidance. We need to see the whole picture. When decisions come from this place, things are different. Even challenges feel different. There is less resentment, less internal conflict, and more ownership of the life being created.

Let's give it a try.

Choosing-In Activity

Audio instructions

1. Sit down.
2. Take a deep breath in through your nose and out through your mouth.
3. Think about a decision you need to make today.
4. Take another deep breath.
5. Consider your options.
6. Take another deep breath.
7. How does one decision feel vs another? Where do you feel it in your body? What is your reaction to that feeling?
8. Take another deep breath.
9. Finalize your decision.

How do you feel about that decision? Did anything come to mind during the pause or the breaths you hadn't thought of before?

"Do not go where the path may lead; go instead where there is no path and leave a trail."

— Ralph Waldo Emerson

Walking

We all know movement is good for us. It's good for our bodies and our minds. Endorphins and all that, right? Right.

But walking is often overlooked because it looks too simple to matter. We are conditioned to associate progress with intensity, which can make gentler forms of movement seem insignificant. Yet walking remains one of the most effective ways to support both physical health and nervous system regulation.

Walking is considered a form of functional fitness, meaning it supports the body's ability to move and function in everyday life. Because it doesn't look dramatic, it's easy to dismiss. But regular walking provides meaningful cardiovascular, metabolic, and mental health benefits.

It is also one of the most accessible forms of movement available. You can do it almost anywhere: at a gym, around a lake, up a mountain, around your neighborhood, or even inside a mall. Some would argue you don't even need shoes (see Grounding Activity).

Walking is about creating space to put your phone down and reconnect with yourself, your surroundings, and the rhythm of your own body in the present moment. Research shows that moderate movement, such as brisk walking for about 150 minutes per week, is associated with significantly lower rates of depression, not because it forces change but because steady, repeatable movement helps regulate the systems that support emotional well-being.

Tie up those laces, let's take a walk.

Walking Activity

Audio instructions

1. Put on your walking shoes.
2. If you can get by without taking your phone, great! If not, bring it, but put it away and don't look at it.
3. No headphones! I know.
4. Go outside.
5. Walk for ten to fifteen minutes.

Can't go outside? Where could you walk for ten to fifteen minutes inside?

Where did you walk? How did that feel? What did you notice?

"Luck is
what happens when
preparation meets
opportunity."

— Lucius Annaeus Seneca

Intention Setting

Some people think intentions are goals or resolutions, but they are not the same thing. Goals focus on outcomes and achievement. Resolutions are generally firm and inflexible. Intentions are when you focus on how you want to show up along the way. They evolve as you grow and situations change.

Intention setting is the practice of identifying what truly matters to you and choosing, day by day, to embody those values in your choices and actions. It's less about forcing a change and more about establishing a guide for you to come back to again and again with awareness and self-compassion.

Research suggests that what we repeatedly focus on strengthens the mental pathways associated with those thoughts and behaviors. In this way, intention setting is less about wishing for change and more about gently training your attention toward what matters most.

When intentions are clear, decisions become less reactive. You begin responding from alignment rather than stress, expectation, or urgency.

The practice is simple: choose one quality or way of being that feels supportive for today. Let's try it!

Intention Setting Activity

Audio instructions

1. Pick an intention or try one of these:
   a. I intend to recognize and appreciate the small things.
   b. I will be kind to myself and others.
   c. Today, I will breathe.
   d. I intend to allow myself to feel my feelings.
2. Stand in front of the mirror, or close your eyes, whichever you prefer.
3. Place your hand on your heart.
4. Slowly say the intention.
5. Pause.
6. Repeat the intention three to five more times, settling into the feeling and calmness of the present moment.
7. Write the intention down, so you can refer to it throughout the day.

Which intention(s) did you choose? ______

How did that feel? What did you notice? Write down any comments, thoughts, or notes you have about the experience. ______

"I am not afraid of storms, for I am learning how to sail my ship."

— Louisa May Alcott

Kindness

Kindness is often treated as something extra, a nice gesture reserved for when we have more time, enough energy, or fewer demands competing for our attention. Research increasingly shows, however, that kindness is a biological and psychological support for well-being.

Small acts of kindness, whether offered to others or extended toward ourselves, have been linked to improved mood, reduced stress, and a stronger sense of connection and belonging. Studies suggest that helping others can decrease feelings of loneliness, increase happiness and self-esteem, and even lower stress hormones such as cortisol while supporting overall health.

Even simple gestures like listening fully, offering encouragement, or helping with a small task can shift emotional perspective and improve well-being for both the giver and the receiver.

Kindness also has a ripple effect. Research shows that when people experience kindness they often spread it to others, encouraging them to act more compassionately themselves. In this way, kindness becomes more than a single action; it becomes a pattern that quietly reshapes our internal and external experience of the world.

Kindness is not about self-sacrifice or giving until we are depleted. Kindness is about how we speak to ourselves and how we care for our own needs.

Sometimes meaningful change begins in one small moment with choosing to respond with kindness instead of from a place of stress.

Kindness Activity

Audio instructions

1. Close your eyes and take a deep breath.
2. Center in on kindness.
3. Choose an act of kindness to complete today. Here are some ideas:
    a. Pay for the person behind you in a drive through.
    b. Text a loved one something nice.
    c. Give someone a compliment.
    d. Smile at a stranger.
    e. Let someone go ahead of you in a line.
    f. Leave a kind note on a stranger's windshield.
    g. Leave a generous tip.
    h. Hold the door open for someone.
    i. Share something you love with someone you love.
    j. Drop off a donation.
    k. Buy some flowers and give them to a stranger.
    l. Offer to help an elderly neighbor or friend.

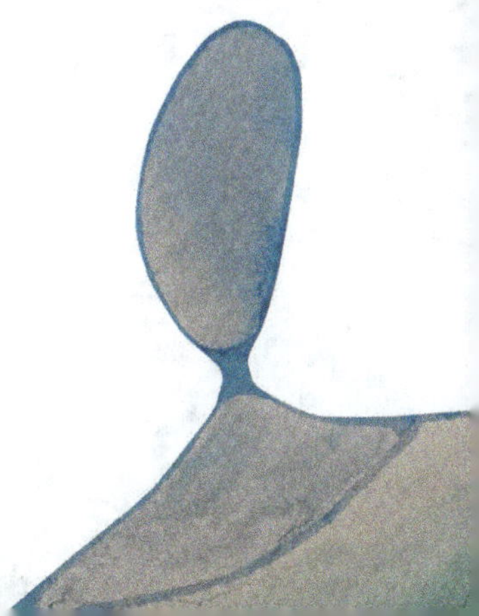

Which act of kindness did you complete?

How did that feel? What did you notice?

"Kindness is the sunshine in which virtue grows."

— Robert Green Ingersoll

30 Days of Curiosity

Now that you've had an opportunity to learn about and experience some new mindfulness activities, it's time to consider getting curious and trying one (or multiple, the sky is the limit) of the activities for thirty days. This is an opportunity to dedicate a few minutes each day to a particular activity to allow you to experience and reflect on how that practice impacts you, over a thirty-day period.

The brain needs repetition to create new neural pathways. Real change and habit creation requires motivation, consistency, and compassion.

What does self-compassion mean to you and do you value it? How can you show yourself more compassion during these days of curiosity?

Telling others about your goals can dramatically increase your chances of success by creating more accountability, providing motivation, and fostering a support system. Sharing with trusted individuals can lead to better performance. People you share with may ask about your progress, offer encouragement and advice, or help you overcome obstacles.

Do you have a person (or two) who would be interested in supporting you on this journey? How could they support you?

"It is never too late to be what you might have been."

— George Eliot

30 Days of Grounding

Now that you've practiced, let's commit! Every day, for thirty days, connect with Mother Earth for ten minutes. Once you got that going, take it up a notch! Do it for fifteen to twenty minutes a day. Like any meaningful change or habit patience and consistency are key.

Too cold to go outside? Try a grounding mat.

Remember, this is a space for curiosity, growth, trying new things, self-compassion and grace. If you start the thirty days and it's just not resonating, it's okay to stop, pause, or adjust as needed.

Rebecca's preferred Grounding Mat

For each day, ask yourself: How did that feel? What did you notice? Any comments, thoughts, or notes about the experience?

Day 1

Day 2

Day 3

Day 4

Day 5

How are you feeling after five days of curiosity?

Day 6

Day 7

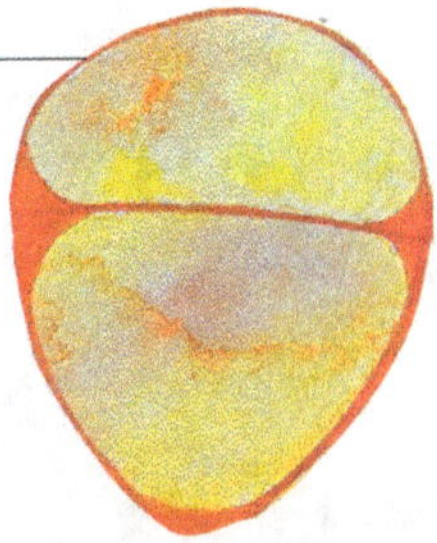

"Just start with showing up."

— HRONN KOLD SIGURDARDOTTIR

Day 8

Day 9

Day 10

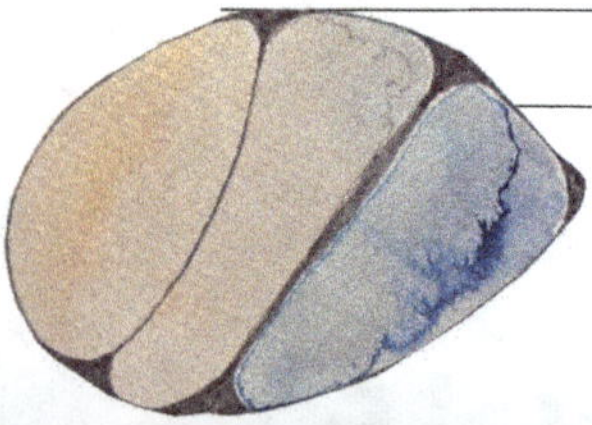

What have you noticed about yourself in the past ten days?

Day 11

Day 12

Day 13

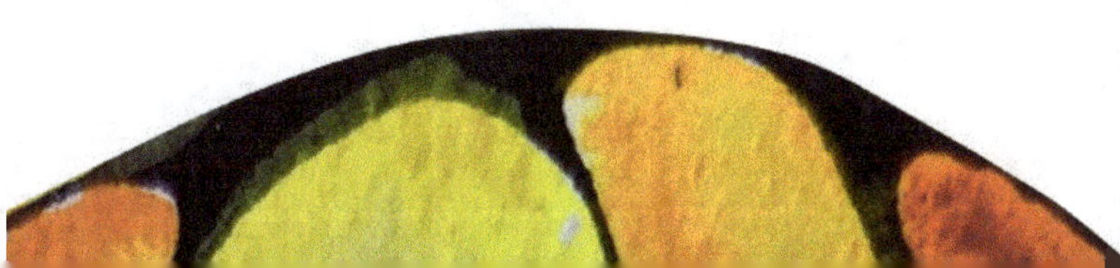

Day 14

"A wise man will make more opportunities than he finds."

— Sir Francis Bacon

Day 15

Day 16

Day 17

Day 18

What is the hardest part so far of completing these thirty days of curiosity? How can you overcome it?

Day 19

Day 20

Day 21

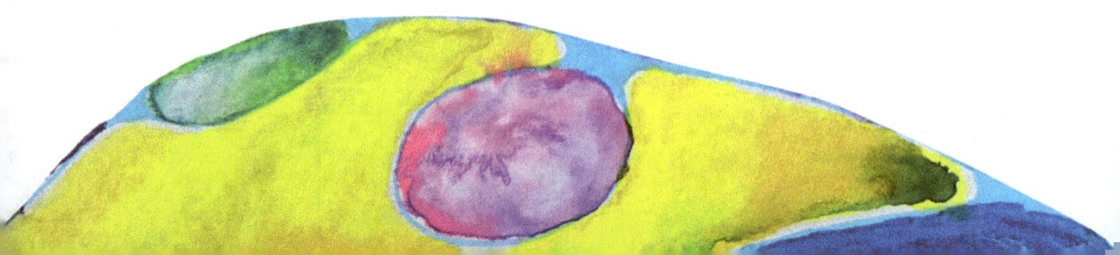

"It does not matter how slowly you go as long as you do not stop."

— Confucius

Day 22

Day 23

Day 24

Day 25

You're twenty-five days in. What might support you in staying with it for the last few days?

Day 26

Day 27

Day 28

"And into the forest I go, to lose my mind and find my soul"

— John Muir

Day 29

Day 30

It's been thirty days. What are you noticing? What has changed? How do you feel? What will you do going forward?

"The highest reward for a person's toil is not what they get for it, but what they become by it."

— John Ruskin

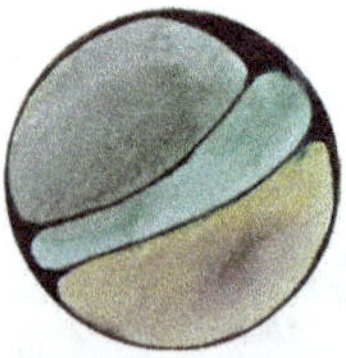

30 Days of Breathing

Now that you've practiced, let's commit! Every day for the next thirty days dedicate a few minutes to your preferred breathing activity.

Once you got that going, take it up a notch! Try a new one, or extend the time on your favorite one.

Remember, this is a space for curiosity, growth, trying new things, self-compassion and grace. If you start the thirty days and it's just not resonating, it's okay to stop, pause, or adjust as needed.

Link to short Wim Hof Guided Breathing video showing different breath practices serve different purposes - some are more activating, others more regulating.

For each day, ask yourself: How did that feel? What did you notice? Any comments, thoughts, or notes about the experience?

Day 1

Day 2

Day 3

Day 4

Day 5

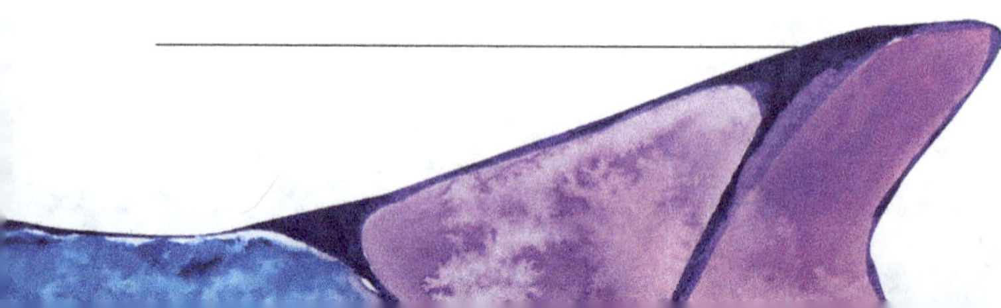

How are you feeling after five days of curiosity?

Day 6

Day 7

"Character cannot be developed in ease and quiet."

— Helen Keller

Day 8

Day 9

Day 10

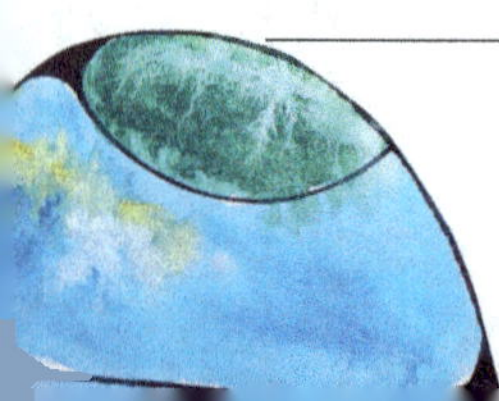

What have you noticed about yourself in the past ten days?

Day 11

Day 12

Day 13

Day 14

> *"Make the best use of what is in your power, and take the rest as it happens."*
>
> — Epictetus

Day 15

Day 16

Day 17

Day 18

What is the hardest part so far of completing these thirty days of curiosity? How can you overcome it?

Day 19

Day 20

Day 21

"If we are to better the future, we must disturb the present."

— Catherine Booth

Day 22

Day 23

Day 24

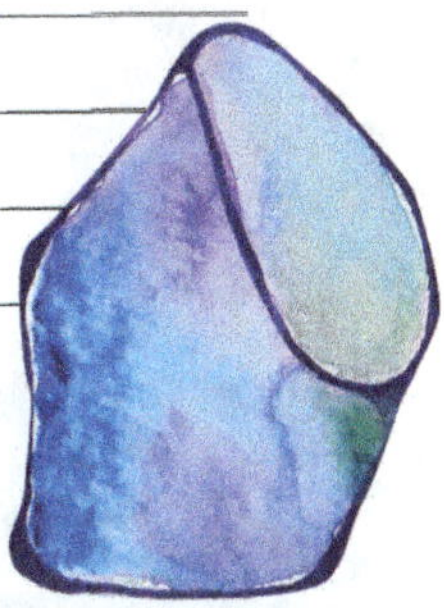

Day 25

You're twenty-five days in. What might support you in staying with it for the last few days?

Day 26

Day 27

Day 28

"Success is the sum of small efforts repeated day in and day out."

— Robert Collier

Day 29

Day 30

It's been thirty days. What are you noticing? What has changed? How do you feel? What will you do going forward?

"You are braver than you believe, stronger than you seem, and smarter than you think."

— A.A. Milne

30 Days of Meditation

Now that you've practiced, let's commit! Every day, for thirty days, dedicate a few minutes to your preferred short meditation activity.

Once you got that going, take it up a notch! Try a new one!

Didn't like the meditations offered here, but still want to step into curiosity? Here are a couple more resources for meditations that I have used.

Remember, this is a space for curiosity, growth, trying new things, self-compassion and grace. If you start the thirty days and it's just not resonating, it's okay to stop, pause, or adjust as needed.

Insight Timer app

Oprah & Deepak Chopra 21 days of gratitude

Deepak Chopra 21 days of abundance

For each day, ask yourself: How did that feel? What did you notice? Write down any comments, thoughts, or notes about the experience.

Day 1

Day 2

Day 3

Day 4

Day 5

How are you feeling after five days of curiosity?

Day 6

Day 7

"Progress is impossible without change, and those who cannot change their minds cannot change anything."

— George Bernard Shaw

Day 8

Day 9

Day 10

What have you noticed about yourself in the past ten days?

Day 11

Day 12

Day 13

Day 14

"The test of life is not in what we get, but in what we become."

— Anna Garlin Spencer

Day 15

Day 16

Day 17

Day 18

What is the hardest part so far of completing these thirty days of curiosity? How can you overcome it?

Day 19

Day 20

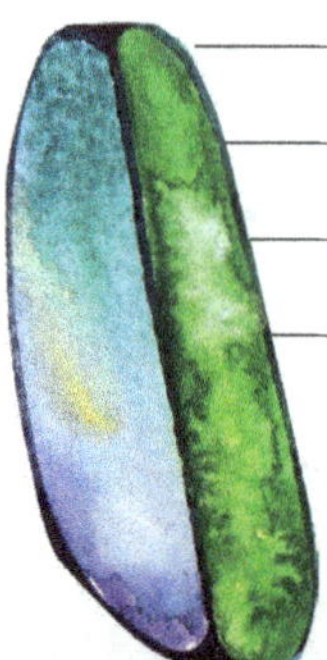

Day 21

"The soul should always stand ajar, ready to welcome the ecstatic experience"

— Emily Dickinson

Day 22

Day 23

Day 24

Day 25

You're twenty-five days in. What might support you in staying with it for the last few days?

Day 26

Day 27

Day 28

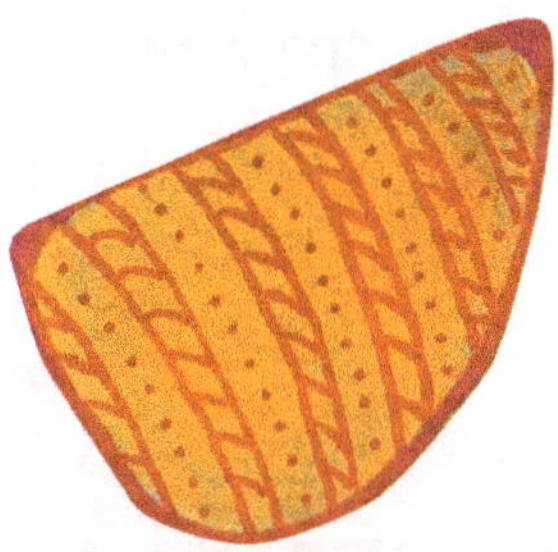

"You have power over
your mind – not outside events.
Realize this, and
you will find strength."

— Marcus Aurelius

Day 29

Day 30

It's been thirty days. What are you noticing? What has changed? How do you feel? What will you do going forward?

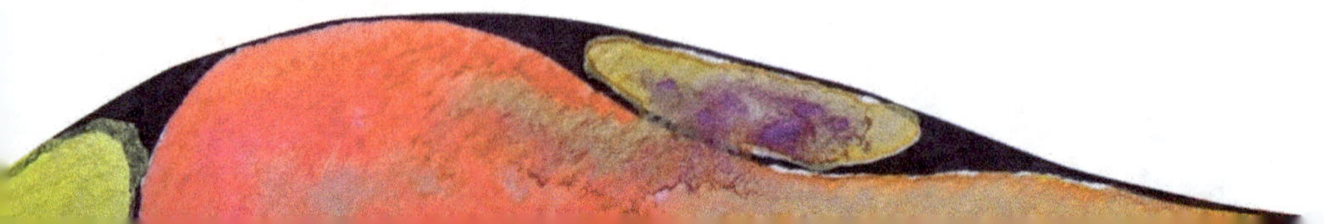

"You were once wild here. Don't let them tame you."

— Isadora Duncan

30 Days of Dance

Now that you've practiced, let's commit! Every day, for thirty days, dance your heart out for at least three minutes (or the length of the song of your choice).

Once you got that going, take it up a notch! Do it twice a day!

Remember, this is a space for curiosity, growth, trying new things, self-compassion and grace. If you start the thirty days and it's just not resonating, it's okay to stop, pause, or adjust as needed.

Rebecca's Dance YouTube Playlist

For each day, ask yourself: How did that feel? What did you notice? Write down any comments, thoughts. or notes about the experience.

Day 1

Day 2

Day 3

Day 4

Day 5

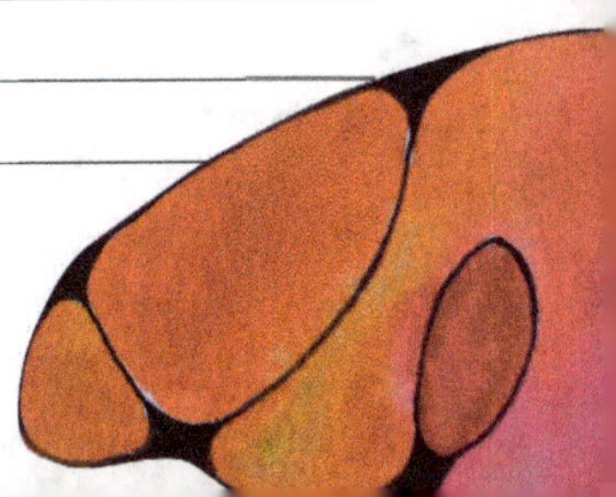

How are you feeling after five days of curiosity?

Day 6

Day 7

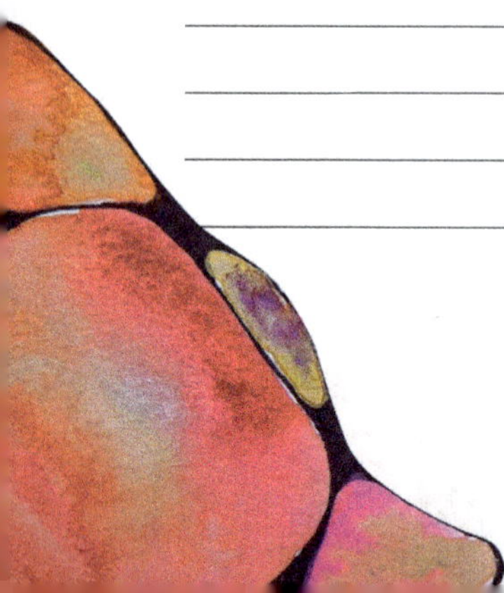

"The most effective way to do it, is to do it."

— Amelia Earhart

Day 8

Day 9

Day 10

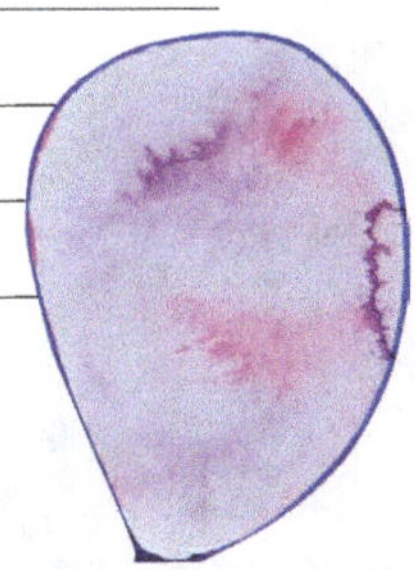

What have you noticed about yourself in the past ten days?

Day 11

Day 12

Day 13

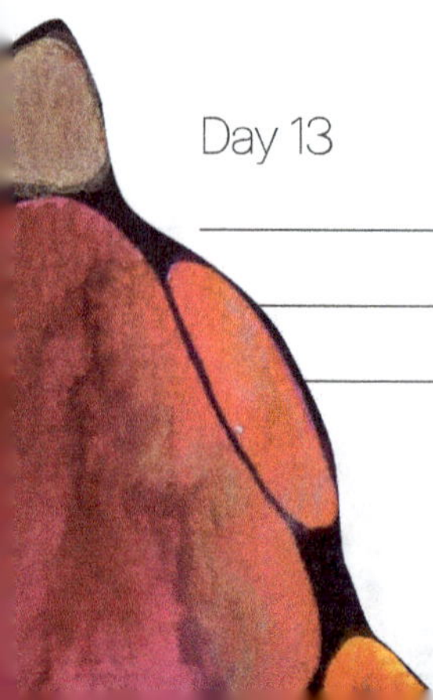

Day 14

"Do the thing you fear,
and the death of
fear is certain."

— Ralph Waldo Emerson

Day 15

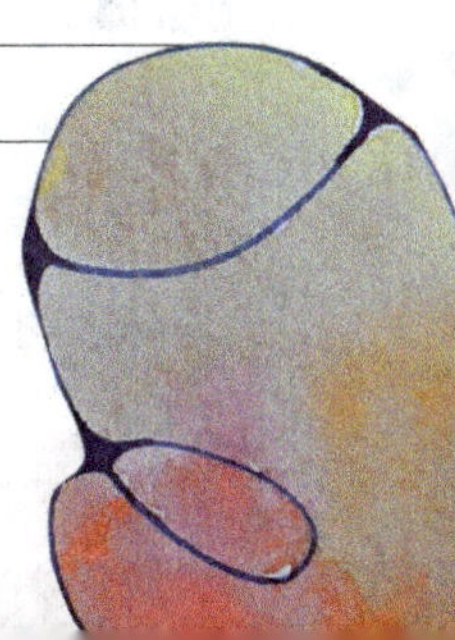

Day 16

Day 17

Day 18

What is the hardest part of completing these thirty days of curiosity? How can you overcome it?

Day 19

Day 20

Day 21

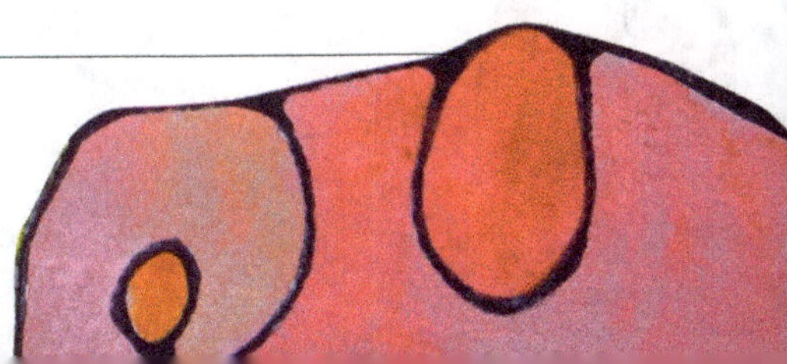

"Dance is the only
art in which we ourselves are
the stuff of which it is made."

— Ted Shawn

Day 22

Day 23

Day 24

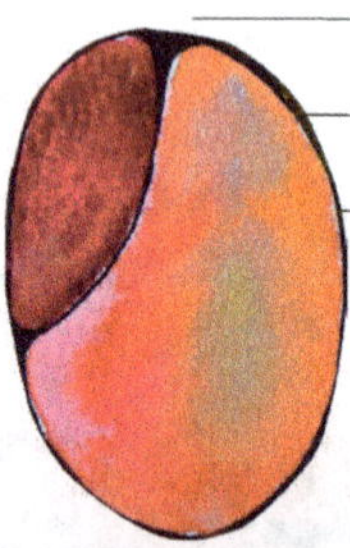

Day 25

You're twenty-five days in. What might support you in staying with it for the last few days?

Day 26

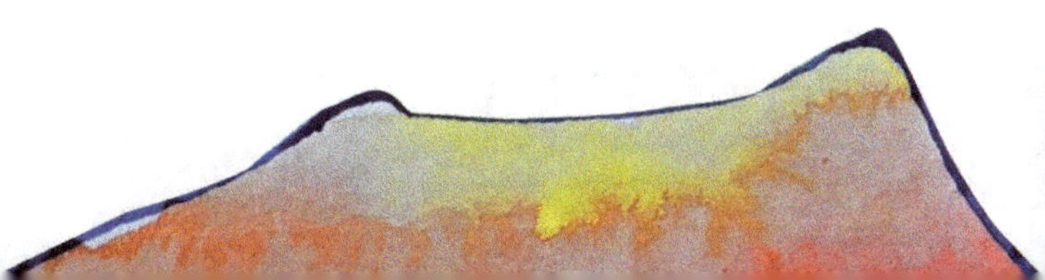

Day 27

Day 28

"If you look the right way, you can see that the whole world is a garden."

— Frances Hodgson Burnett

Day 29

Day 30

It's been thirty days. What are you noticing? What has changed? How do you feel? What will you do going forward?

"Go as far as you can see; when you get there, you'll be able to see farther."

— Thomas Carlyle

30 Days of Gratitude

Now that you've practiced, let's commit! Every day, for thirty days, think about and write down three to five things you are grateful for.

When during the day, you ask? Whenever feels right. When you wake up, to start your day. Before bed, to end your day in a positive way.

Once you got that going, take it up a notch! Add more to that list!

If three to five is too many, start with one and work your way up.

Remember, this is a space for curiosity, growth, trying new things, self-compassion and grace. If you start the thirty days and it's just not resonating, it's okay to stop, pause, or adjust as needed.

Day 1

I AM GRATEFUL FOR: ______________________________

Day 2

I AM GRATEFUL FOR: ______________________________

Day 3

I AM GRATEFUL FOR:

Day 4

I AM GRATEFUL FOR:

Day 5

I AM GRATEFUL FOR:

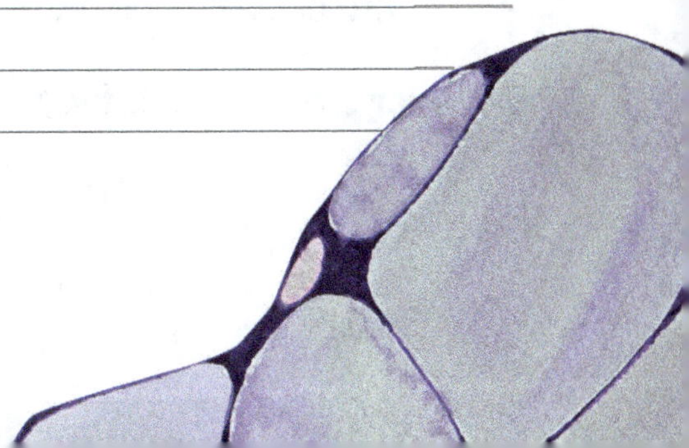

How are you feeling after five days of curiosity?

Day 6

I AM GRATEFUL FOR:

Day 7

I AM GRATEFUL FOR:

"Gratitude is not only the greatest of virtues, but the parent of all others."

— CICERO

Day 8

I AM GRATEFUL FOR:

Day 9

I AM GRATEFUL FOR:

Day 10

I AM GRATEFUL FOR:

What have you noticed about yourself in the past ten days?

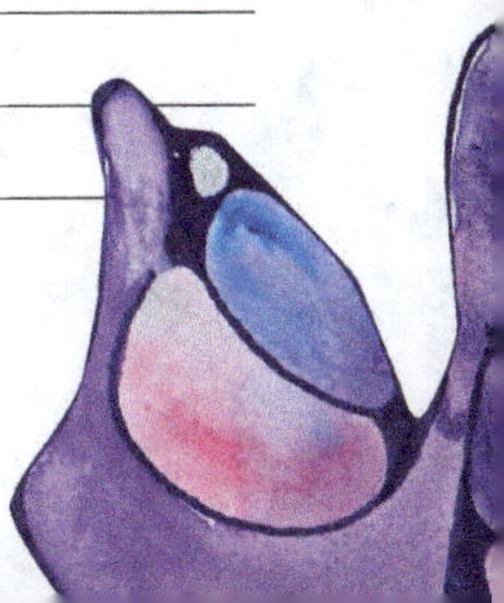

Day 11

I AM GRATEFUL FOR:

Day 12

I AM GRATEFUL FOR:

Day 13

I AM GRATEFUL FOR:

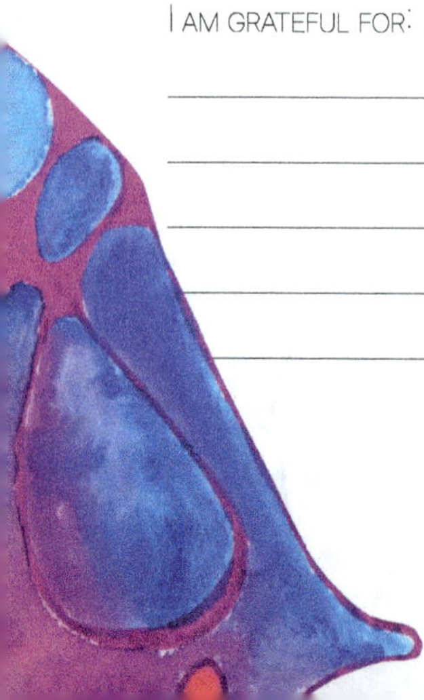

Day 14

I AM GRATEFUL FOR:

"There is no chance, no destiny, no fate, that can hinder the firm resolve of a determined soul."

— ELLA WHEELER WILCOX

Day 15

I AM GRATEFUL FOR:

Day 16

I AM GRATEFUL FOR:

Day 17

I AM GRATEFUL FOR:

Day 18

I AM GRATEFUL FOR:

What is the hardest part of completing these thirty days of curiosity? How can you overcome it?

Day 19

I AM GRATEFUL FOR:

Day 20

I AM GRATEFUL FOR:

Day 21

I AM GRATEFUL FOR:

"The soul that gives thanks can find comfort in everything."

— HANNAH WHITALL SMITH

Day 22

I AM GRATEFUL FOR:

Day 23

I AM GRATEFUL FOR:

Day 24

I AM GRATEFUL FOR:

Day 25

I AM GRATEFUL FOR:

You're twenty-five days in. What might support you in staying with it for the last few days?

Day 26

I AM GRATEFUL FOR:

Day 27

I AM GRATEFUL FOR:

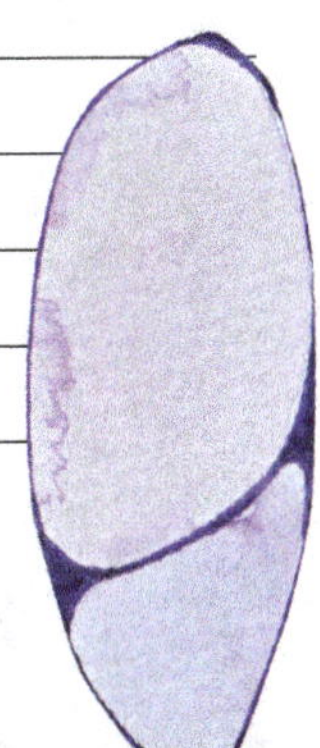

Day 28

I AM GRATEFUL FOR: ______

"It is never too late to be what you might have been."

— George Eliot

Day 29

I AM GRATEFUL FOR: ______

Day 30

I AM GRATEFUL FOR: ______

It's been thirty days. What are you noticing? What has changed? How do you feel? What will you do going forward?

"Never give up, for that is just the place and time that the tide will turn."

— Harriet Beecher Stowe

30 Days of Coloring

Now that you've practiced, let's commit! Every day, for thirty days, spend ten to fifteen minutes coloring. You can use the following images or your favorite coloring book, or even your own sketch pad!

If ten to fifteen minutes is too much, try five. Make it more accessible for yourself.

Didn't finish coloring from the day before? Go back to that one and don't worry about starting the next day just yet.

Don't like one of the coloring pages? Skip it!

Once you got that going, take it up a notch! Add some more time, or try some new tools. If you used colored pencils, what about colored pens?

Remember, this is a space for curiosity, growth, trying new things, self-compassion and grace. If you start the thirty days and it's just not resonating, it's okay to stop, pause, or adjust as needed.

Day 1

Day 2 - Grand Canyon

Day 3 - Design by Shannon

Day 5 - Crowley Lake

How are you feeling after five days of curiosity?

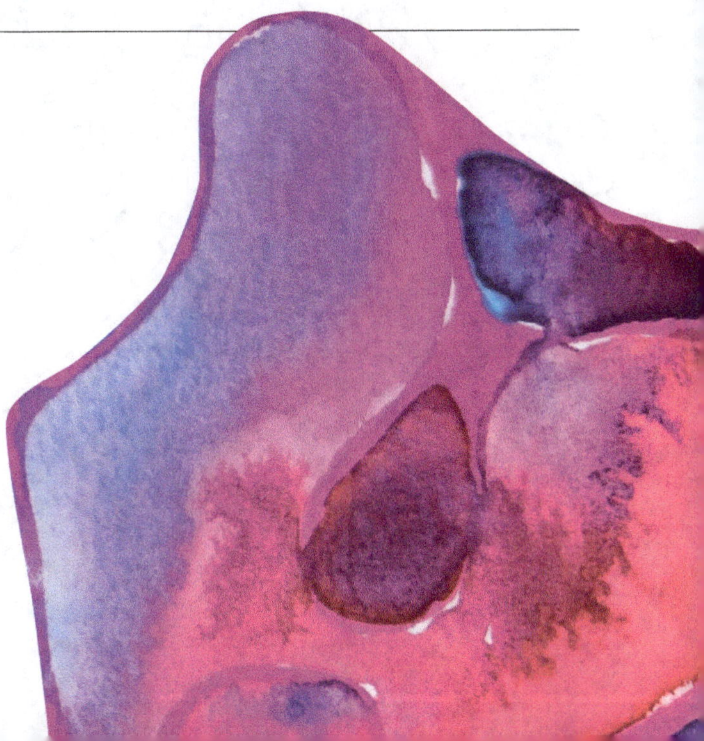

Day 6 - Design by Zak Weinberg (@grebniew_kaz)

Day 7 - Lake Tahoe

"The more we do, the more we can do."

— Maria Edgeworth

Day 8 - Virginia City

Day 9

Day 10 – Redwoods

What have you noticed about yourself in the past ten days?

Day 11 - Design by Shannon

Day 12 - Cooper Creek Reservoir

Day 13

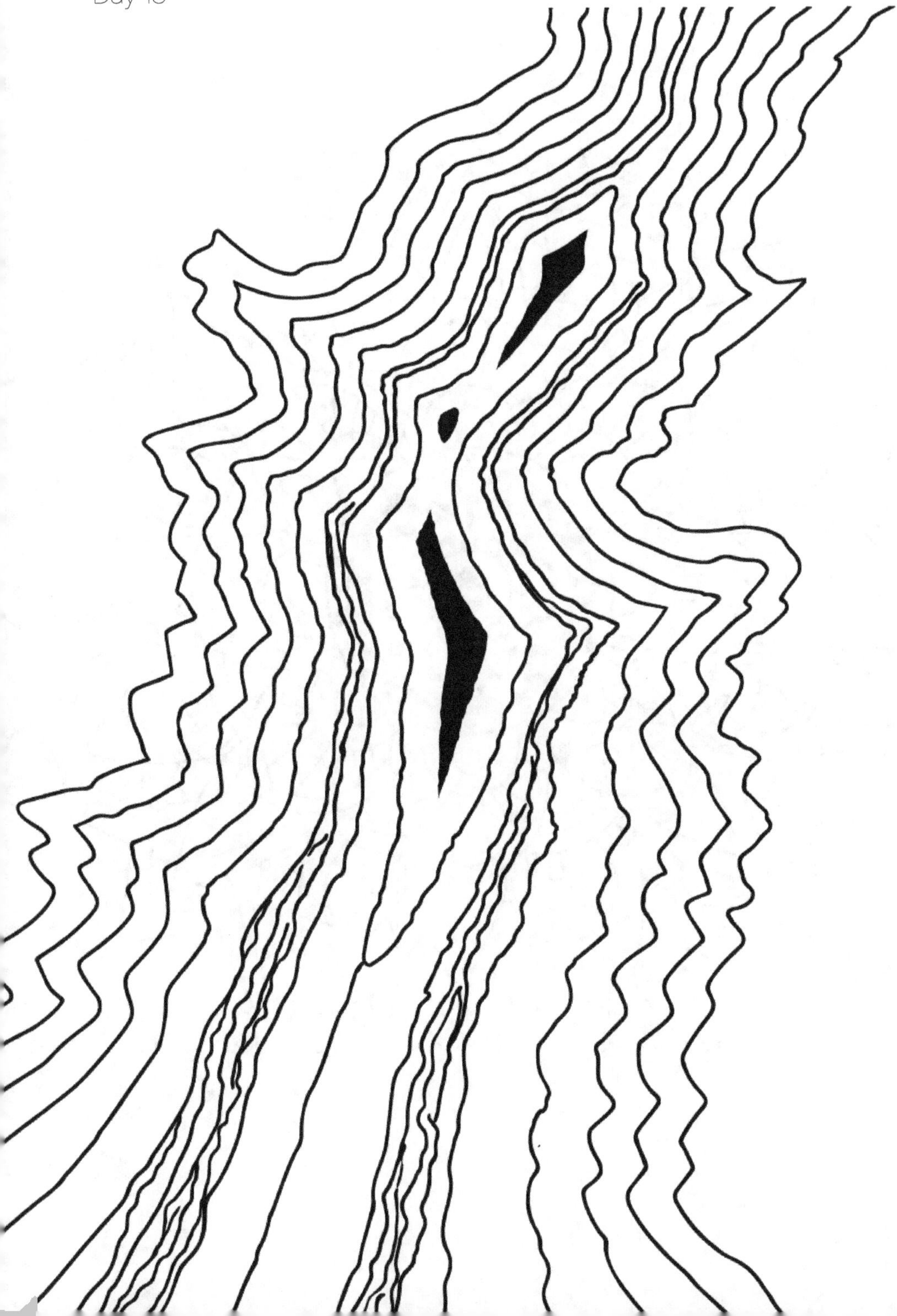

Day 14 - Design by Shannon

"We do not learn to be artists by sitting in galleries."

— Anna Jameson

Day 15 – Leavenworth

Day 16 - The Bray

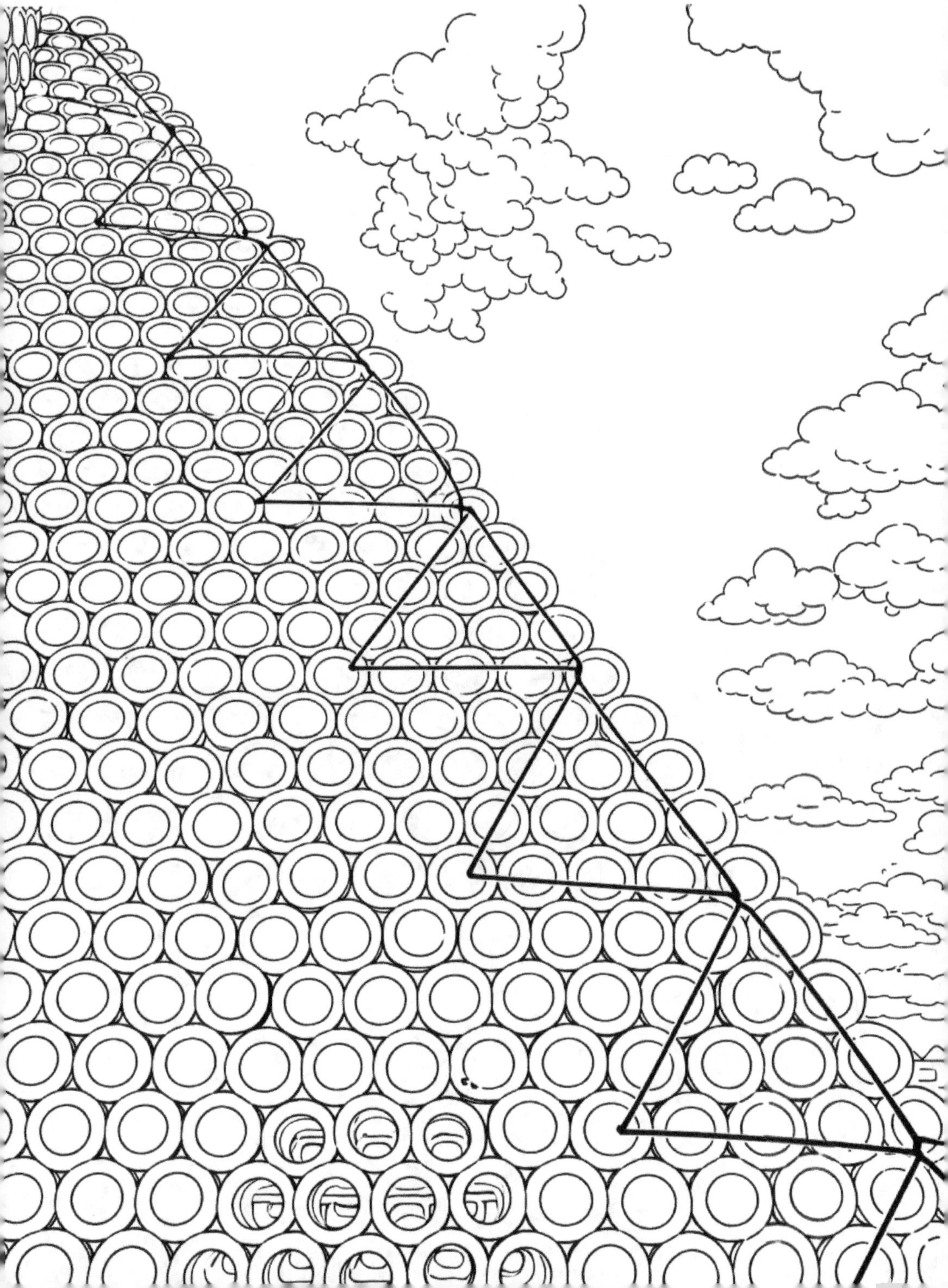

Day 17 – Design by Brian Geckle (@briangeckleart)

Day 18 - Yellowstone

What is the hardest part of completing these thirty days of curiosity? How can you overcome it?

Day 19 - Circle of Sacred Smoke

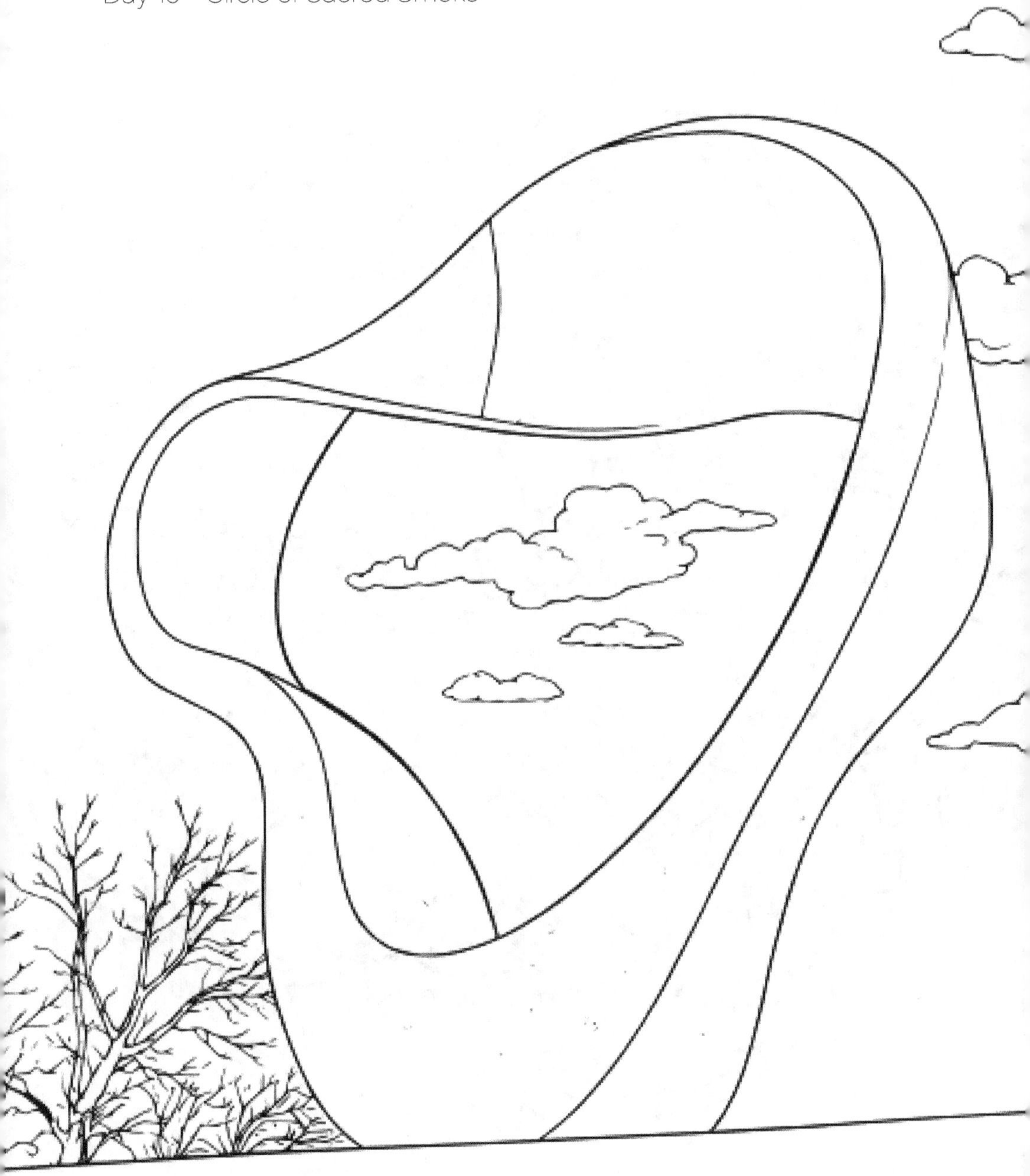

Day 20 - Design by Shannon

Day 21

"Great things
are done by
a series of
small things
brought together."

— Vincent Van Gogh

Day 22 - Dignity Statue

Day 23 - Otter Lake

Day 24 - Design by Shannon

Day 25 - Cincinnati Zoo

You're twenty-five days in. What might support you in staying with it for the last few days?

Day 26 - Design by Brian Geckle (@briangeckleart)

Day 27 - Gulf of Mexico

Day 28 - Design by Shannon

"Truth is strong, and sometime or other will prevail."

— Mary Astell

Day 29 - Design by Brian Geckle (@briangeckleart)

Day 30

It's been thirty days. What are you noticing? What has changed? How do you feel? What will you do going forward?

"The greatest achievement was at first and for a time a dream."

— James Allen

30 Days of Mindful Eating

Now that you've practiced, let's commit! Every day, for thirty days, commit to two to four mindful bites of any food, a meal, a snack, whatever.

Once you got that going, take it up a notch! Add some more bites, or more times during the day, or even a dedicated mindful snack or meal! What about for four to five minutes at one time?

Remember, this is a space for curiosity, growth, trying new things, self-compassion and grace. If you start the thirty days and it's just not resonating, it's okay to stop, pause, or adjust as needed.

For each day, ask yourself: How did that feel? What did you notice? Any comments, thoughts, or notes about the experience?

Day 1

____

____

____

____

____

____

Day 2

____

____

____

____

Day 3

Day 4

Day 5

How are you feeling after five days of curiosity?

Day 6

Day 7

"We mostly spend our lives conjugating three verbs: to want, to have, and to do."

— Evelyn Underhill

Day 8

Day 9

Day 10

What have you noticed about yourself in the past ten days?

Day 11

Day 12

Day 13

Day 14

"Knowing is not enough; we must apply. Willing is not enough; we must do."

— Johann Wolfgang Von Goethe

Day 15

Day 16

Day 17

Day 18

What is the hardest part of completing these thirty days of curiosity? How can you overcome it?

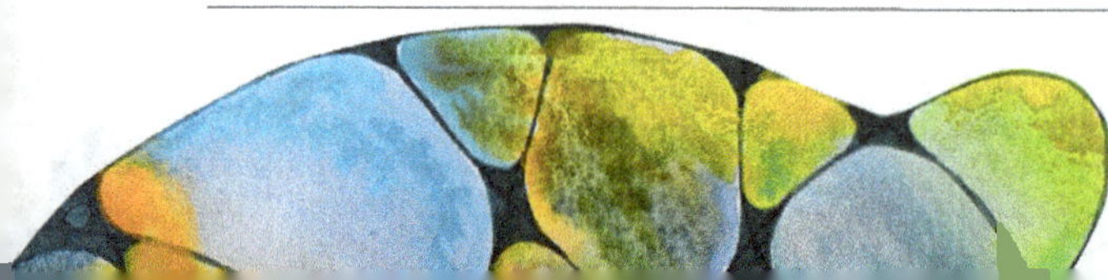

Day 19

Day 20

Day 21

"The secret of change is to focus all of your energy not on fighting the old, but on building the new."

— Socrates

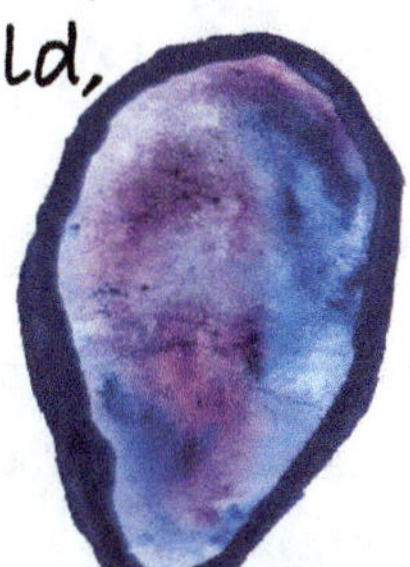

Day 22

Day 23

Day 24

Day 25

You're twenty-five days in. What might support you in staying with it for the last few days?

Day 26

Day 27

Day 28

"There are two ways of spreading light: to be the candle or the mirror that reflects it."

— Edith Wharton

Day 29

Day 30

It's been thirty days. What are you noticing? What has changed? How do you feel? What will you do moving forward?

"When I let go of what I am, I become what I might be."

— Lao Tzu

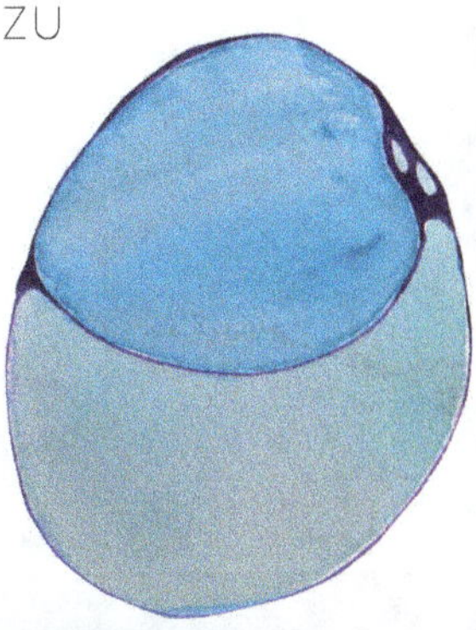

30 Days of Affirmations

Now that you've practiced, let's commit! Every day, for thirty days, commit to repeating an affirmation. It can be the same affirmation every day, or you can choose to change it up if something doesn't resonate with you.

Once you got that going, take it up a notch and say a few!

Not sure where to start? **The Mind Body Dictionary**, QR code below, has a plethora of connected and intuitive affirmations.

Remember, this is a space for curiosity, growth, trying new things, self-compassion and grace. If you start the thirty days and it's just not resonating, it's okay to stop, pause, or adjust as needed.

For each day, ask yourself: How did that feel? What did you notice? Any comments, thoughts. or notes about the experience?

Day 1

AFFIRMATION:

NOTES:

Day 2

AFFIRMATION:

NOTES:

Day 3

AFFIRMATION:

NOTES:

Day 4

AFFIRMATION:

NOTES:

Day 5

AFFIRMATION:

NOTES:

How are you feeling after five days of curiosity? ____________

____

____

____

____

____

____

Day 6

AFFIRMATION: ____________________________________

____

____

NOTES: ____

____

____

____

____

____

Day 7

AFFIRMATION: ____________________________________

____

____

NOTES: ____

____

____

____

____

____

"The bravest thing
you can do
when you are not
brave is to profess
courage and act
accordingly."

— Corra Harris

Day 9

Affirmation: ______________________________

____

____

Notes: ______________________________

____

____

____

____

____

Day 10

Affirmation: ______________________________

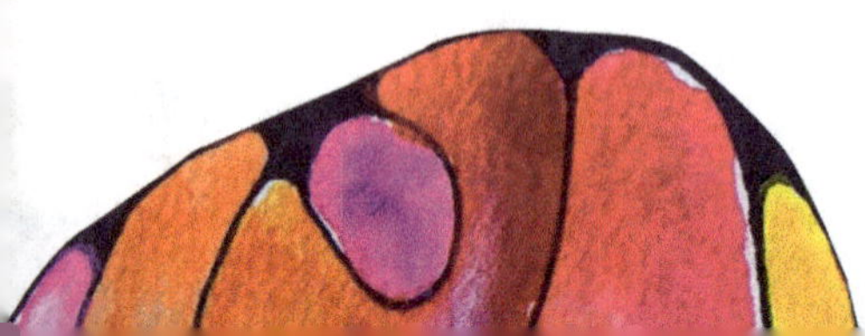

NOTES:

What have you noticed about yourself in the past ten days?

Day 11

AFFIRMATION:

NOTES:

Day 12

AFFIRMATION: ____________________

____

____

NOTES: ____________________

____

____

____

____

____

Day 13

AFFIRMATION: ____________________

____

____

NOTES: ____________________

____

____

____

____

____

Day 14

AFFIRMATION: ____________________

____

____

NOTES: ____________________

____

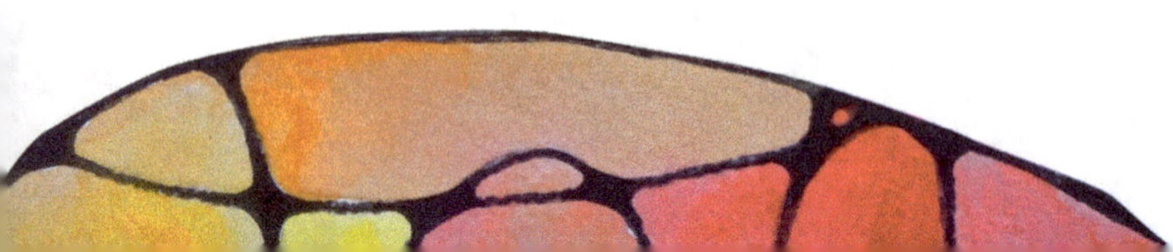

"A man is literally what he thinks, his character being the complete sum of all his thoughts."

—-James Allen

Day 15

Affirmation: __________

Notes: __________

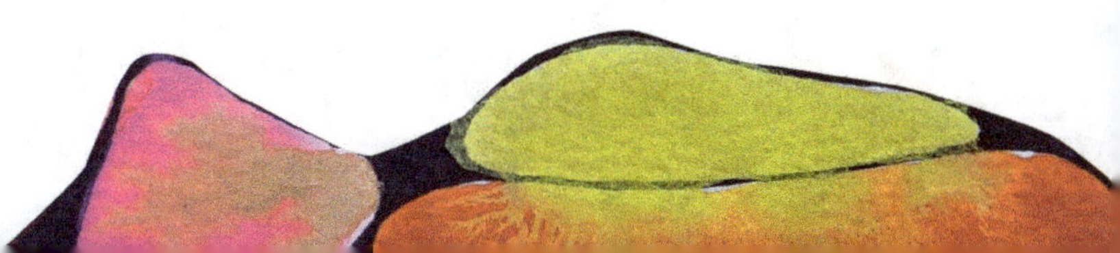

Day 16

AFFIRMATION: ______

NOTES: ______

Day 17

AFFIRMATION: ______

NOTES: ______

Day 18

AFFIRMATION: ______

NOTES: ______

What is the hardest part of completing these thirty days of curiosity? How can you overcome it? ______

Day 19

AFFIRMATION: ______

NOTES: ______

Day 20

AFFIRMATION: ______

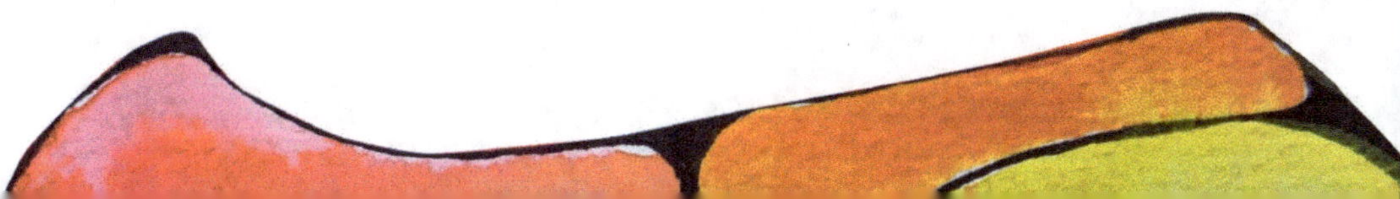

NOTES: ______________________________

____

____

____

____

____

Day 21

AFFIRMATION: ______________________________

____

____

NOTES: ______________________________

____

____

____

____

____

"The whole character is shaped by the thoughts we dwell upon."

— FRANCES POWER COBBE

Day 22

AFFIRMATION: ______________________________

____

____

NOTES:

Day 23

AFFIRMATION:

NOTES:

Day 24

AFFIRMATION:

NOTES:

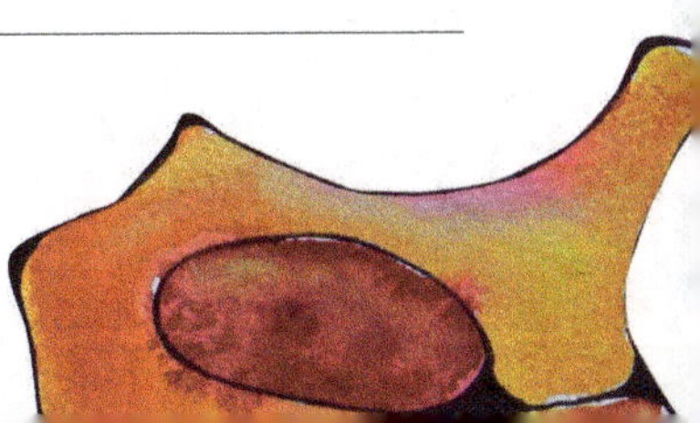

Day 25

AFFIRMATION: ____________________

NOTES: ____________________

You're twenty-five days in. What might support you in staying with it for the last few days? ____________________

Day 26

AFFIRMATION: ____________________

NOTES: ____________________

Day 27

AFFIRMATION:

NOTES:

Day 28

AFFIRMATION:

NOTES:

"Let everything happen to you: beauty and terror. Just keep going. No feeling is final."

— Rainer Maria Rilke

Day 28

Affirmation: ______________________________

____

____

Notes: ______________________________

____

____

____

____

____

Day 29

Affirmation: ______________________________

____

____

Notes: ______________________________

____

____

____

____

____

Day 30

AFFIRMATION:

NOTES:

It's been thirty days. What are you noticing? What has changed? How do you feel? What will you do going forward?

"To attain happiness in another world we need only to believe something, while to secure it in this world we must do something."

— Charlotte Perkins Gilman

30 Days of Choosing In

Now that you've practiced, let's commit! Every day, for thirty days, commit to consciously choosing-in (or out) at least once a day the pause, the intuition and/or analysis, and the conscious choice.

Once you got that going, take it up a notch! Try to do it more than once a day.

Remember, this is a space for curiosity, growth, trying new things, self-compassion and grace. If you start the thirty days and it's just not resonating, it's okay to stop, pause, or adjust as needed.

For each day, ask yourself: What did you choose in (or out) to? How did that feel? What did you notice? What came up in the pause, or the breaths, that didn't before when you thought about this choice? Any comments, thoughts, or notes about the experience?

Day 1

____

____

____

____

____

____

Day 2

Day 3

Day 4

Day 5

How are you feeling after five days of curiosity?

Day 6

Day 7

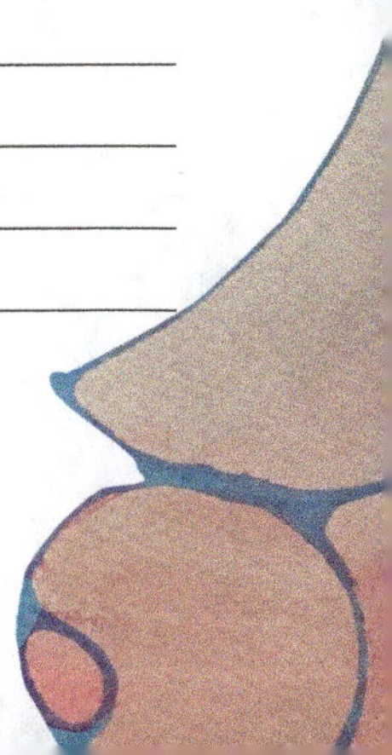

"It is always the simple that produces the marvelous."

— Amelia Barr

Day 8

Day 9

Day 10

What have you noticed about yourself in the past ten days?

Day 11

Day 12

Day 13

Day 14

"*Action may not always bring happiness, but there is no happiness without action.*"

— Benjamin Disraeli

Day 15

Day 16

Day 17

Day 18

What is the hardest part of completing these thirty days of curiosity? How can you overcome it?

Day 19

Day 20

Day 21

"Nothing could be worse than the fear that one had given up too soon."

— Jane Addams

Day 22

Day 23

Day 24

Day 25

You're twenty-five days in. What might support you in staying with it for the last few days?

Day 26

Day 27

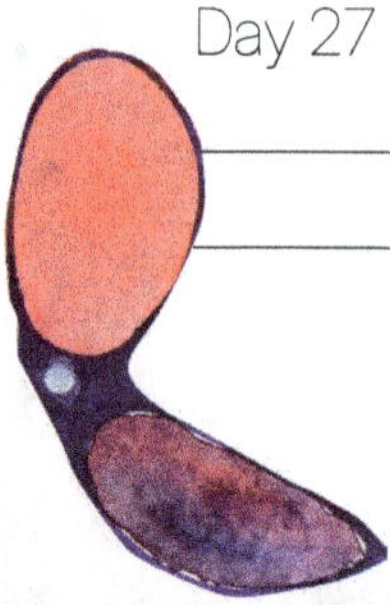

Day 28

"Out of difficulties grow miracles."

— Jean de La Bruyère

Day 29

Day 30

It's been thirty days. What are you noticing? What has changed? How do you feel? What will you do moving forward?

"Life can only be understood backwards; but it must be lived forwards."

— Søren Kierkegaard

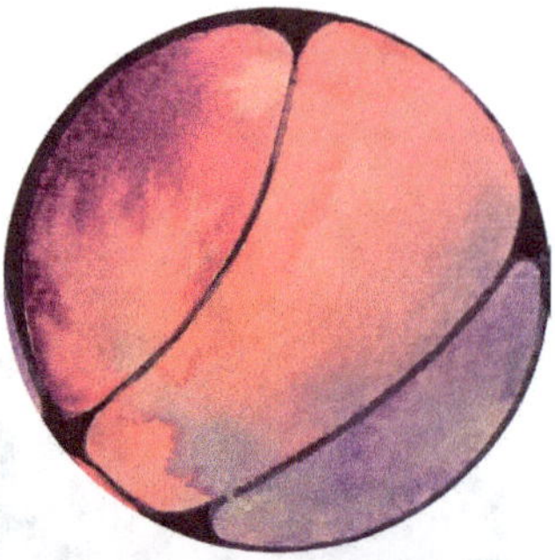

30 Days of Intention Setting

Now that you've practiced, let's commit! Every day, for thirty days, commit to consciously setting an intention for the day.

An intention is a conscious decision about how you choose to show up. It is a gentle direction for your attention and energy, chosen with awareness.

Remember, this is a space for curiosity, growth, trying new things, self-compassion and grace. If you start the thirty days and it's just not resonating, it's okay to stop, pause, or adjust as needed.

For each day, ask yourself: How did that feel? What did you notice? Any comments, thoughts, or notes about the experience?

Day 1

INTENTION____

NOTES ____

Day 2

INTENTION

NOTES

Day 3

INTENTION

NOTES

Day 4

INTENTION

NOTES

Day 5

INTENTION

NOTES

How are you feeling after five days of curiosity?

Day 6

INTENTION

NOTES

Day 7

INTENTION

NOTES

"Light tomorrow with today."

— Elizabeth Barrett Browning

Day 8

INTENTION

NOTES

Day 9

INTENTION

NOTES

Day 10

INTENTION

NOTES

What have you noticed about yourself in the past ten days?

Day 11

INTENTION

NOTES

Day 12

INTENTION

NOTES

Day 13

INTENTION

NOTES

Day 14

INTENTION

NOTES

"The best of life is but intention well applied."

— Eliza Cook

Day 15

INTENTION

NOTES

Day 16

INTENTION

NOTES

Day 17

INTENTION

NOTES

Day 18

INTENTION

NOTES

What is the hardest part of completing these thirty days of curiosity? How can you overcome it?

Day 19

INTENTION

NOTES

Day 20

INTENTION

NOTES

Day 21

INTENTION

NOTES

"Either I will find a way,
or I will make one."

— Philip Sidney

Day 22

INTENTION______________________________

NOTES ______________________________

Day 23

INTENTION______________________________

NOTES ______________________________

Day 24

INTENTION__________

NOTES __________

Day 25

INTENTION__________

NOTES __________

You're twenty-five days in. What might support you in staying with it for the last few days?

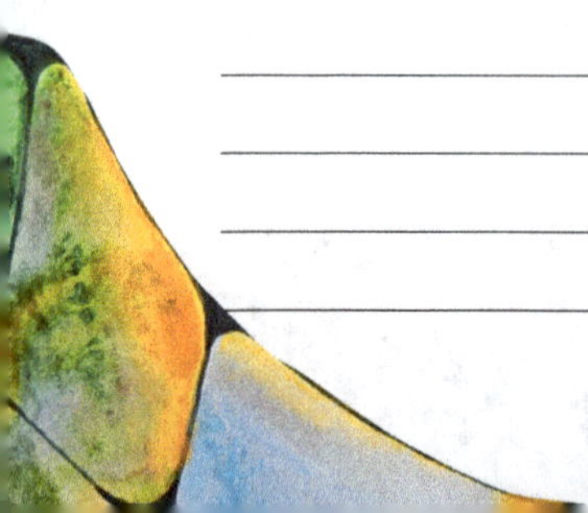

Day 26

INTENTION

NOTES

Day 27

INTENTION

NOTES

Day 28

INTENTION

NOTES

> "The mind will ever be unstable that has only prejudices to rest on."
>
> — Mary Wollstonecraft

Day 29

INTENTION

NOTES

Day 30

INTENTION

NOTES

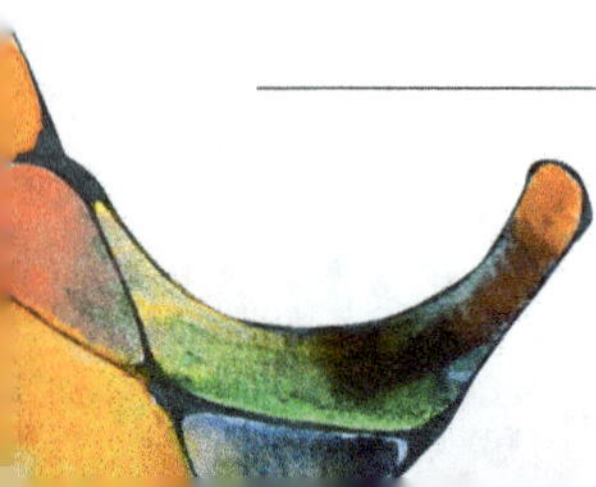

It's been thirty days. What are you noticing? What has changed? How do you feel? What will you do going forward?

"Be who you were meant to be and you will set the world on fire."

— St. Catherine of Siena

30 Days of Kindness

Now that you've practiced, let's commit! Every day, for thirty days, commit to consciously participating in an act of kindness towards another person.

Refer back to the activity for some initial ideas. Here are a few more:

1. Check in on someone you haven't heard from in a while.
2. Offer a genuine apology where it's needed, maybe even to yourself.
3. Give someone your full, undivided attention in a conversation.
4. Do something kind for your future self (prep a meal, tidy your space, set something up for tomorrow).

Remember, this is a space for curiosity, growth, trying new things, self-compassion and grace. If you start the thirty days and it's just not resonating, it's okay to stop, pause, or adjust as needed.

For each day, ask yourself: How did that feel? What did you notice? Any comments, thoughts, or notes about the experience?

Day 1

ACT OF KINDNESS ______________________________

____

____

NOTES______________________________

____

____

Day 2

ACT OF KINDNESS

NOTES

Day 3

ACT OF KINDNESS

NOTES

Day 4

ACT OF KINDNESS

NOTES

Day 5

ACT OF KINDNESS

NOTES

How are you feeling after five days of curiosity?

Day 6

ACT OF KINDNESS

NOTES

Day 7

ACT OF KINDNESS

NOTES

"Kindness is a language which everyone understands."

— James Freeman Clarke

Day 8

ACT OF KINDNESS

NOTES

Day 9

ACT OF KINDNESS

NOTES

Day 10

ACT OF KINDNESS

NOTES

What have you noticed about yourself in the past ten days?

Day 11

ACT OF KINDNESS

NOTES

Day 12

ACT OF KINDNESS

NOTES

Day 13

ACT OF KINDNESS

NOTES

Day 14

ACT OF KINDNESS

NOTES

"The smallest act of kindness is worth more than the grandest intention."

— Oscar Wilde

Day 15

ACT OF KINDNESS ______________________________

____

____

NOTES______________________________

____

____

____

____

____

Day 16

ACT OF KINDNESS ______________________________

____

____

NOTES______________________________

____

____

____

____

____

Day 17

ACT OF KINDNESS

NOTES

Day 18

ACT OF KINDNESS

NOTES

What is the hardest part of completing these thirty days of curiosity? How can you overcome it?

Day 19

ACT OF KINDNESS

NOTES

Day 20

ACT OF KINDNESS

NOTES

Day 21

ACT OF KINDNESS

NOTES

“The surest proof of wisdom is kindness.”

— Elizabeth Carter

Day 22

ACT OF KINDNESS

NOTES

Day 23

ACT OF KINDNESS

NOTES

Day 24

ACT OF KINDNESS

NOTES

Day 25

ACT OF KINDNESS

NOTES

You're twenty-five days in - what might support you in staying with it for the last few days? ______________________

Day 26

ACT OF KINDNESS ______________________

NOTES ______________________

Day 27

ACT OF KINDNESS ______________________

NOTES ______________________

Day 28

ACT OF KINDNESS

NOTES

"It is love alone that gives worth to all things."

— Teresa of Ávila

Day 29

ACT OF KINDNESS

NOTES

Day 30

ACT OF KINDNESS

NOTES

It's been thirty days. What are you noticing? What has changed? How do you feel? What will you do going forward?

"Happiness consists not in having, but in being."

— Henry Drummond

Bonus Content

30 additional days of curiosity – Walking

30 additional days of curiosity – Everyday Awareness

More info about the paintings in this journal (Neurographic paintings)

Notes

1. Stephen T. Sinatra, Drew S. Sinatra, Stephen W. Sinatra, Gaetan Chevalier, "Grounding – The universal anti-inflammatory remedy," *Biomedical Journal*, Volume 46, Issue 1 (2023): 11-16, https://doi.org/10.1016/j.bj.2022.12.002.
2. Jill Bolte Taylor, *My Stroke of Insight: A Brain Scientist's Personal Journey* (Penguin Books, 2009).
3. Bruno Bordoni, Shahin Purgol, Annalisa Bizzarri, Maddalena Modica, Bruno Morabito, "The Influence of Breathing on the Central Nervous System," 2018, https://pmc.ncbi.nlm.nih.gov/articles/PMC6070065/.
4. Susan I Hopper, Sherrie L Murray, Lucille R Ferrara, Joanne K Singleton, "Effectiveness of diaphragmatic breathing for reducing physiological and psychological stress in adults: a quantitative systematic review," 2019, https://pubmed.ncbi.nlm.nih.gov/31436595/.
5. Fox, G. R., Kaplan, J., Damasio, H., & Damasio, A. (2015). *Neural correlates of gratitude. Frontiers in Psychology*, 6, 1491.
6. Christopher N Cascio, Matthew Brook O'Donnell, Francis J Tinney, Matthew D Lieberman, Shelley E Taylor, Victor J Strecher, Emily B Falk, "Self-affirmation activates brain systems associated with self-related processing and reward and is reinforced by future orientation," 2015, https://pmc.ncbi.nlm.nih.gov/articles/PMC4814782.